THE CINEMA OF POWELL AND PRESSBURGER

Edited by

Nathalie Morris & Claire Smith

THE BRITISH FILM INSTITUTE
Bloomsbury Publishing Plc
50 Bedford Square, London, WC1B 3DP, UK
1385 Broadway, New York, NY 10018, USA
29 Earlsfort Terrace, Dublin 2, Ireland
BLOOMSBURY is a trademark of Bloomsbury Publishing Plc

First published in Great Britain 2023 by Bloomsbury
on behalf of the
British Film Institute
21 Stephen Street, London W1T 1LN
www.bfi.org.uk

The BFI is the lead organisation for film in the UK and the distributor of Lottery funds for film. Our
mission is to ensure that film is central to our cultural life, in particular by supporting and nurturing
the next generation of filmmakers and audiences. We serve a public role which covers the cultural,
creative and economic aspects of film in the UK.

Cover design by Louise Dugdale
Front cover image: Costume sketch for *The Tales of Hoffmann* (1951) by Ivor Beddoes
(© Ivor Beddoes/© STUDIOCANAL/BFI National Archive)
Back cover image: Production design for *The Red Shoes* (1948) by Ivor Beddoes
(Ivor Beddoes/©ITV/BFI National Archive).

A catalogue record for this book is available from the British Library.

A catalog record for this book is available from the Library of Congress.

ISBN: HB: 978-1-8387-1917-3
ePDF: 978-1-8387-1915-9
eBook: 978-1-8387-1916-6

Project managed and designed by Tom Cabot/ketchup

Printed and bound in India

To find out more about our authors and books visit
www.bloomsbury.com/bfi and sign up for our newsletters.

Contents

A Letter from Tilda Swinton

Dear P & P,

I'm writing to you from somewhere down the track, round a corner or two, but nonetheless in the clearest ear and eyeshot.

Micky, I am the girl Sally Potter brought to you down the lane at Avening one spring day in the late 1980s; you listened so generously to our dreams of filming an 'unfilmable' book. We wanted to be bandits and we knew you'd understand it. You infected us with your glee at the challenge and the warmth of your encouragement felt like an ancestral blessing.

Later, you wrote a wee script, a music video for New Order – *The Sands of Dee* – and somewhere in the eaves of my house is a one-page treatment under the magical embossed Archers' logo with a scene involving a high shot from a cliff of a girl on a Scottish beach, and the immortal suggestion: 'Maybe if Tilda has her own dog she can bring him/her …'

And I'm the one who brought a pocket of sand in my handkerchief from a Scottish beach and poured it and a sprig of heather from your Hebrides into your resting place. You could say, in the bonkers bus station of life, we just about connected.

Emeric, we never met down here, but that doesn't mean a thing, as we know: you are my Conductor, as you are for countless others, up and down the Stairway to Heaven and across all seas, up all mountains, through all whirlpools, all storms.

I think the weather was one of the first things I fell in love with in your films: the way that storms bring transformation into and out of people's sense of their own stories, the way in which people are constantly being blown off course and slap bang into their lives. The inexplicable forces of the natural world, the mystical – pagan – properties of destiny and premonition … your territory is borderless and your skies are freedom itself.

I can't exactly say which of the Archers' films I saw first. I can't, frankly, remember a time when I hadn't seen a P&P film. Beside the fireplace in the Potts drawing room in *I Know Where I'm Going!* is a map of the isle of Kiloran, in fact, recognisably the island of Colonsay which I have known all my life and happens to be pretty much my favourite place on earth. My sleeper train journeys north have always, to this day ever since I was a child, been accompanied by that lambent lullaby and sped through that dream landscape of valleys between tartan hills … *IKWIG* is the film I wear pinned to my heart possibly most closely: it is the film I declare most readily when asked the always tricky question about what my favourite film might be. It feels like part of the story of my life.

And then, in a different way, so does *A Matter of Life and Death*. When facing a sudden – and eventually happily avoidable – operation in a neurological hospital in my thirties, my mind (inside my poor head) filled with images of David Niven's vast papier-mâché eyelid slowly closing into oblivion, accompanied by the remorseless chords of Allan Gray's theme as my own stairway trundled heavenwards, I was informed – my hand on my heart, here – that my neurosurgeon would be a Mr M. Powell.

And, to push the point one stop further, the family I grew up in contained, for at least the generations I am familiar with, a succession of well-meaning, somewhat arcane, variously idealistic and moustachioed generals whose combined biography is meticulously described in the one *The Life and Death of Colonel Blimp*. Beyond which, the heavenly Roger Livesey shares the same sandy, upright, wholesome optimistic innocence of heart I recognise as cousin.

You Archers: your pirate soul on the high seas of cinema is everlastingly buoyant. Yours is a contribution beyond all rubies. That emphatic banner: thudding arrows into Spitfire straw with its heady two-scoop flavour combo of essential Anglo Saxon chivalry – both jousting knights and vagabond outlaws – is pure and perpetual magic in its promise of epic adventure, verve and heart.

Consistently referred to as perhaps the most quintessentially English of filmmaking families, we nonetheless recognise as unmistakably essential to your universe a peerless production design born out of the luxurious glamour of continental European expressionism, the smoke and mirrors of the theatre, the opera and the mark of the hand painted, hand wrought, hand made. In harmony with the Magyar romanticism and highly evolved humanism of Emeric Pressburger, we have, then, England at her very best, maybe: inclusive, passionate, radical, highly cultured, irreverent, open hearted, fun. And built independently by comrades in step and with shared clarity of purpose towards high ends. This example of fellowship in action is a never-ending beacon for us all, from all corners.

> The arrow was pure gold
> But somehow missed the target
> But, as all Golden Arrow trippers know
> 'Tis better to miss Naples than hit Margate.[1]

On the path of my still nascent life as a filmmaker, the breadcrumbs I follow were dropped by you. And the film I never made with Michael Powell and my own dog, is among my proudest achievements.

With love and heartfelt thanks for the light, for the dance, for the horizon.

See you later,

Tilda

---

1. The rhyme attributed to critic James Agate that inspired the name of The Archers. Cited by Michael Powell, *A Life in Movies* (London: Faber & Faber, 2000), 387.

Emeric Pressburger and Michael Powell on location in Monte Carlo for *The Red Shoes* (1948). (© ITV/BFI National Archive)

A Letter from Michael Powell to Emeric Pressburger

Tuesday

Dear Imre

It is very calm here. I do nothing except work with my hands and browse upon books as far removed as possible from reality. I think a good deal. The unwonted exercise makes me sleep better.

This is almost the first time that I have been able to pause and consider our friendship. How lucky we have been! What struggles we have shared and what happiness it has been to struggle and succeed together at just the time when we can do our best work. 'Funny how the war can open your eyes to a lot of things.'

I am sorry about the play. I think it might have been a success if brought to London but Hemingway is out of luck. You have been a real friend and partner all through. I have learnt a great deal and I only hope it will be of use to us in other times: and it isn't only about the theatre that I have learnt a lesson.

I walked yesterday to the North Coast near Lynton: the Valley of Rocks and Woody Bay, fantastic and Doré-esque scenery. The sea was so calm that not even on the rocky shore was there any movement. The cliff road is a thousand feet above the sea there and you look down on the sea-birds flying below. I saw ravens and buzzards as well as gulls. The coast looks like Corfu and yesterday there was a light haze over the landscape, making luminous colours on the cliffs and a flat milky sheet over the sea so that the coast of Wales floated like a mirage along the horizon. This might be the setting for the exterior scenes with the young airman: it could have been any country, here or hereafter; and, further along where the coast flattens, there is a great American camp.

"A Matter of Life and Death"! It has style – 'very much style'.

I have thought over your opinions and fears of the future. I don't think that these fears are for us, except to urge us to make more and better pictures. We can't change other people except by our own example. And it seems to me we must worry first about our own spiritual growth – there will be enough material things to hinder that anyway.

I must rush to catch the post.

Love

Micky.

Letter from Michael Powell to Emeric Pressburger, reflecting on their partnership and sharing ideas for *A Matter of Life and Death* (1945), undated. (© Michael Powell/BFI National Archive)

Design for the tapestry in the opening credits of *The Life and Death of Colonel Blimp* (1943) by Ivor Beddoes. (Ivor Beddoes/©ITV/BFI National Archive)

The tapestry featured in the opening credits of *The Life and Death of Colonel Blimp* (1943) by The Royal School of Needlework. (Private Collection)

1

Introduction

Nathalie Morris and Claire Smith

T he opening titles of Powell and Pressburger's *The Life and Death of Colonel Blimp* (1943) show a heraldic tapestry in muted colours. A walrus-moustached Clive Wynne-Candy (the titular 'Blimp' character, played by Roger Livesey) – wrapped in a bath towel and bearing a spear – sits astride a white horse as he trots past an ancient oak. The oak is styled as an elaborate family tree, bearing in its leaves a handful of the names that came to make up the production family known as 'the Archers'.

Tapestry, as an art form, is a fittingly ancient and steadfast choice for a film that views 'the changing world of the last forty years through the eyes of one unchanging man'.[1] *The Life and Death of Colonel Blimp* follows Wynne-Candy from his beginnings as a dynamic young officer to his frustrations in older age. The unusual, episodic structure presents discreet windows into Wynne-Candy's life, revealing his struggles to come to terms with modern warfare and his pursuit of a near-mystical romantic ideal. In a nod to the eternal feminine, all three love interests are played by the same actor, Deborah Kerr. Typically for Powell and Pressburger, a clear sense of magic underlies the authentic textures of everyday life.

It's no coincidence that Powell and Pressburger chose tapestry to preface a production that they both named as a favourite and decisive film within their partnership. Tapestry is an allegorical craft of the mind and the hand, bound up in visual storytelling since

---

1. Michael Powell, draft letter to Wendy Hiller (n.d., but early 1942), reproduced in *Powell and Pressburger, The Life and Death of Colonel Blimp*, ed. Ian Christie (London: Faber and Faber, 1994), 17.

Arachne first wove her threads in defiance of the Greek gods. Here it underlines a form of narrative that is never linear, but always has both a warp and a weft. The tapestry was a bespoke 'make', stitched by the Royal School of Needlework and based on an original cartoon by Archers' sketch artist Ivor Beddoes. Much more than a metaphor, it profiles craft and nods to the universe of physical things that are imagined and made before and beyond film. It is a type of filmmaking that is unafraid to show the marks of its making and to highlight those people who made it. (See figures facing previous page.)

So while on the surface this is a book about film, it is also a book about craft and about people. At its heart sit many more of these evocative talismans; the archives of the Archers, which encompassed some of the most influential visual stylists and storytellers of the Twentieth Century.

The Archers didn't appear in name until 1942, but they began in spirit when British director Michael Powell first collaborated with Hungarian screenwriter Emeric Pressburger on *The Spy in Black* (1939). It would be the first of 19 feature films created by these two men and the talented web of collaborators that they brought together. All films were rich in passion, invention and fantasy. From 1942 onwards, Powell and Pressburger adopted the distinct and now legendary credit, 'Written, Produced and Directed By' and incorporated their production company, the Archers, the following year. While collaborative partnerships were not new to British cinema of the 1940s (the Boulting Brothers, and Launder and Gilliat were both active and successful in these years), Powell and Pressburger's shared credit most certainly was. It defined their practice. Both had significant (and in many ways ground-breaking) careers separate from this collaboration, but it is the films they made together until the disbandment of the Archers in 1957 that really changed the landscape of cinema. These were some of the biggest films of their day, including *The Life and Death of Colonel Blimp* (1943), *A Canterbury Tale* (1944), *I Know Where I'm Going!* (1945), *A Matter of Life and Death* (1946), *Black Narcissus* (1947), *The Red Shoes* (1948), *The Small Back Room* (1949) and *Gone to Earth* (1950).

The aesthetic of an Archers' production is often defined by its romanticism and bravery, inserting a mystical, Technicolor door into the subdued palette of war-torn Europe. But it is also fundamentally an aesthetic through which the details of each screen art – cinematography, design, editing, music, choreography and much more – can be read. Each film has a combinatory quality that celebrates its component parts: an elegant hybridity that is all the more beautiful for its daring embrace of wide-reaching artistic styles.

In many ways, the Archers worked more like a traditional theatrical company than a film production unit. As Raymond Durgnat has outlined in more detail, Powell and

Pressburger 'fit awkwardly into film theory, since Powell, though a true *auteur*, often thought more like an impresario, or a producer, who draws ideas from a team of collaborators.'[2] The scene in *The Red Shoes*, in which Lermontov and his composer, choreographer, designer and performers come together to create their ballet production can serve as a shorthand representation of their process and beliefs. A collective practice that was as fulfilling and transformative as the productions themselves.

Their process was unusually intimate and familial, but by no means small. A glance at the budget sheets reveals just how many creatives were involved. Amongst these, composers Allan Gray and Brian Easdale created scores that were haunting, lyrical, humorous and experimental, depending on the requirements of the project. Easdale's contribution was particularly important to Powell's notion of the 'composed film': the harmonious synthesis of sound and vision. Powell continued to work with Easdale as he branched out without Pressburger in the 1950s. Powell's diary entries of this period are filled with collaborative meetings with Easdale and others (pp. 20–5), and give a deeply personal insight into what he saw in those around him.

Cinematographers Erwin Hillier and Jack Cardiff made striking contributions, bringing very different but equally important qualities to the Archers' films. Hillier, an Ufa-trained master of black and white lighting, created some of the most achingly beautiful and magical moments in film history (think of the train dream sequence, Joan's counting of the beams and the chiaroscuro landscapes of *I Know Where I'm Going!*). Picking up where cinematographer Georges Périnal left off with *The Life and Death of Colonel Blimp*, Jack Cardiff (who had been Technicolor cameraman on that film), pushed Technicolor in new directions with *A Matter of Life and Death*, *Black Narcissus* and *The Red Shoes*. In turn, Cardiff's talented camera operator Chris Challis became an accomplished cinematographer in his own right, stepping up to the role first on the Archers' production *The End of the River* (1947) and then becoming Powell and Pressburger's cinematographer from *The Small Back Room* (1949) onwards.

David Lean was a valued editor on *49th Parallel* (1941) and *One of Our Aircraft is Missing* (1942), but Powell and Pressburger's key editors were John Seabourne and then Reginald Mills. Seabourne had worked with Powell since his quota quickie days, and in Powell's words 'his contribution to our films was immense and varied'.[3] Reginald Mills took up the

---

2.   Raymond Durgnat, 'The Powell and Pressburger Mystery', *Cineaste* 23.2 (1997), 16.

3.   Michael Powell, *A Life in Movies* (London: Faber & Faber, 1986), 533.

reins from *A Matter of Life and Death* onwards, and stayed with the Archers until 1956's *The Battle of the River Plate*. His long-time assistant editor Noreen Ackland worked alongside him on some of Archers' greatest films before getting her first editor credit on Powell's *Peeping Tom* in 1960.

Special effects pioneer W. Percy Day, credited with some of the greatest innovations in early visual effects, worked with the Archers throughout the 1940s. His technical wizardry and meticulous draughting skills helped Powell and Pressburger to pull off many of their most daring feats, including *Black Narcissus'* central conjuring of the Indian Himalayas on the backlot of Pinewood Studios – all with the deliberate hints of irreality commanded by the narrative. Eric Gray, Fred Daniels and George Cannons stepped in as regular Powell and Pressburger stills photographers. Powell himself started his career this way, creeping around the set of Hitchcock's *Champagne* (1928) to carefully restage key moments from the production. He continued to hold the art of stills photography in high regard, presenting a London exhibition on the subject in 1948, with his own collaborators very much at the heart of it.

Production designer Alfred Junge, costume and production designer Hein Heckroth, and regular art director Arthur Lawson (alongside countless sketch artists and draughts-men), used their skills to create iconic, artificial, neo-Romantic worlds, first in dramatic black and white and then saturated in jewel-like Technicolor, encompassing everything from a modernist heaven to dark and fantastical ballets where reality and artifice collide. Junge and Heckroth were both political émigrés who brought with them a Continental design sensibility. Junge was one of the earliest Archers' collaborators. A consummate professional, he brought elegant restraint to the set and formality to the production floor. Each production was as immaculately realised as his conté wash drawings. Heckroth first worked with Powell and Pressburger as a costume designer, before taking on both produc-tion and costume design from *The Red Shoes* onwards. Heckroth's painterly and surrealist designs marked a new way of working for Powell and Pressburger and one that brought them closer to the composed film. Heckroth's synthesis of spatial, temporal, photographic and bodily performance closely aligned the production with the balletic principles of sym-metry, dynamic balance and harmony.

Other Archers who worked behind the scenes but were long-standing and essential members of the team included production secretaries Betty Curtis and Joan Page, publi-cist Vivienne Knight and Powell's friend and personal assistant, Bill Paton.

The films stand in testimony to the collective skills of these individuals. Evidence of their professional working lives is sometimes harder to trace, but a few named archives weave their way in and out of public view, offering a way into the many partnerships and friendships that made the Archers unique. These archives, like stories and people, are migratory. Nearly all are well-travelled border-crossers that carry tales of their makers' movements across the continents, and have now settled throughout the world. They represent the way in which each individual has challenged boundaries, both national and disciplinary, in the pursuit of creativity. They are cross-pollinated with cultural influences and ideas, and are full of echoes of the past. In their archived state, they also continue to perform for new audiences, articulating questions about collaboration, artistry, identity and belonging that still resonate to this day.

The archives of Michael Powell and Emeric Pressburger now reside at the BFI National Archive. As is the case for their working partnership, they stand as individual statements of near-boundless creativity, as well as forming an intricately linked duet of conversations, thoughts and reflections. Michael Powell's archive stretches from the juvenilia that he wrote as a teenager through to the very last years of his life, thanks to the dedicated efforts of his widow, Thelma Schoonmaker, to preserve the archive in its entirety. Over half of it relates to unrealised projects – a tantalising glimpse into what might have been. In later life Powell also started to mentor a new generation of filmmakers, including Martin Scorsese (whose Film Foundation has played a key part in restoring many of their films, in collaboration with the BFI and other film archives around the world) and Francis Ford Coppola, who hired Powell as 'director in residence' at his Zoetrope Studios in the 1980s. Even earlier, Josef von Sternberg and Cecil B. DeMille were famous fans. Powell's archive reflects these relationships: a powerful legacy that reaches beyond the canon of Powell and Pressburger films. Other directors to admire or be inspired by their work include Sally Potter, Guillermo del Toro, Wes Anderson, P. T. Anderson, Joanna Hogg and Bong Joon-ho, as well as artist filmmakers including Derek Jarman, Su Friedrich, Alex Prager and Michelle Williams Gamaker.

Pressburger's archive stretches from his early career in Berlin, through to the solo projects that he undertook in later life. Like Powell, the majority of the archive reflects the key decades of their work with the Archers. Just as many shelves are dedicated to unrealised projects; ideas for films, books and plays. Pressburger's correspondence can be business-like (as with so many working papers, the economics of production reverberate throughout). The tone can be frustrated or elated, but at all times it demonstrates the profound respect that these men had for each other, and their belief that they could truly transform the art of film. In amongst letters and production papers are Pressburger's treatments. Invariably by hand, often in pencil or sometimes fountain pen on notepaper, this is where Pressburger's personality is most apparent. By all accounts a self-effacing man, Pressburger's treatments, in contrast, are animated and expressive. Passed backwards and forwards between the two men during the development of a project, the scripts that emerged were key tools within their collaboration: assembling collective ideas, evolving Pressburger's words through Powell's eyes, making marks that made worlds. These scripts are the backbone of Pressburger's archive.

A name that is lesser-known but who forms a key part of the BFI National Archive is Ivor Beddoes. A sketch and storyboard artist, matte painter, costume and set designer, painter, dancer, composer, choreographer and poet, Beddoes worked as a scenic artist under Junge, honing his skills amongst the innovative techniques of *Black Narcissus*, before working as an artist and assistant designer alongside Heckroth. With a chameleon-like ability, Beddoes adapted to the aesthetic of each production, generating many hundreds of drawings. His archive gives a real sense of how the Archers' visual vocabulary evolved. His drawings can be sites of power, order and knowledge, but also of spontaneity, disobedience and joy. Full of the marks and traces of others, they chart the many hands and minds involved in production and show how the Archers' definitive statements on art were all built on a paper premise. They are at once personal musings on a subject, and collective tools of communication within the studio system, performing a number of key functions. They facilitated creative exchanges between collaborators, and chart the evolution of tone, atmosphere, meaning and creative direction. They show what might have been, as well as what ultimately emerged.

Just as the Archers were made up of many voices, so too, is this publication. The films are only one part of what constitutes their cinema, so the themes explored in this publication emerge from an initial reading of the archives now cared for by the BFI; an attempt to encompass the complexity of Powell and Pressburger through concepts driven by the papers themselves. Given the body of existing scholarship, the book does not offer an exhaustive consideration of each theme. Instead, it draws on a range of contributors – film and literary scholars, novelists – to take us deep into each idea, illustrated with archival works from key Archers collaborators. And taking their cue from Powell and Pressburger, authors do not follow a chronology but move backwards and forwards through time, sometimes touching on similar moments from different perspectives.

Exiles and outsiders populate Caitlin McDonald's chapter. McDonald takes us through the early years and making of the Archers, with a particular focus on Emeric Pressburger as an émigré and enemy alien, and the lasting impact this had on his work. Alexandra Harris travels through Powell and Pressburger's filmed lands, both real and imagined, following inadvertent pilgrims on journeys tinged with magic and myth in a way that ultimately transforms their lives.

Selecting the breathtaking *Black Narcissus* (1947) as his focal point, Mahesh Rao considers the film and its source text from an Anglo-Indian perspective. As the first chapter to concentrate on a single production, Rao presents a very personal reading of the material, with a particular focus on the actor Sabu. Looking at the legacy of *Black Narcissus* over 60 years later, Rao shows how its commitment to art and artifice still leaves a powerful, and sometimes troubling, impression.

Colour, Sarah Street leads us to conclude, is both emotion and location in Powell and Pressburger's cinema. Drawing out the contributions of Jack Cardiff and Hein Heckroth, Street leads us through a cinematic space where the technical and expressive aspects of colour collide. Ian Christie tackles the many optical motifs in Powell and Pressburger's films. Mirrors, magic lanterns, camera obscuras, cameras and lenses, trompe l'oeil, the subjective camera, spectacles and eyes, are all used to play with our perceptions, delight our senses, and make us reflect upon our role as cinematic spectators.

In a fitting end to the book, Marina Warner leads us through the genesis of Powell and Pressburger's most famous and enduring statement on art, *The Red Shoes*. With one blood-stained foot in the film's literary roots, Warner takes us from Hans Christian Andersen's fairy tale through to the ultimate filmic ballet.

Warner's chapter points out how Powell and Pressburger made themselves part of a much wider conversation on literature, art, music and dance, encompassing a wide and eclectic array of source materials and pushing the artistic boundaries of film and its crafts. They pursued filmmaking in its widest form. The resultant films have gone on to demonstrate an enduring hold on the collective imagination. For this reason, a number of contemporary voices have been invited to speak for themselves within the publication. These are creative professionals drawn from across the arts. None feel the need to slavishly mirror the practices of Powell and Pressburger in their work, but all share Powell and Pressburger's desire to cross boundaries. From production designer Sarah Greenwood to milliner Stephen Jones, these are artists pushing the envelope of their creative practice. Together, they suggest how Powell and Pressburger took the first bold, imaginative steps on an artistic journey that continues to this day. It is clear that three quarters of a century on from the height of their partnership, the work of Powell and Pressburger continues to inspire and intrigue some of the most fascinating minds working today.

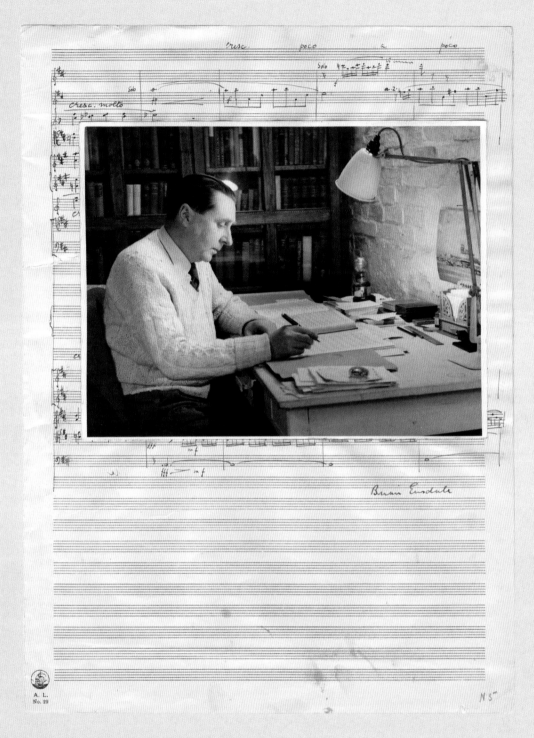

Brian Easdale photographed at work in his study, against an example of Easdale's sheet music. (Brian Easdale/ BFI National Archive)

A Note on Collaboration

Thelma Schoonmaker Powell

n 1952, Michael Powell started keeping a diary. It had been a year since he had directed a film (*The Tales of Hoffmann*). The British film industry was in crisis, and for the first time Powell found time to keep a diary each day, which he did until the end of his life. He and Emeric Pressburger had now left the Rank Organisation, in part due to Rank's refusal to promote *The Red Shoes* (1948). They also found collaborating with Alexander Korda increasingly constraining, working on projects over which they had no final control. Powell was particularly excited to plan a daring series of films in collaboration with famous artists in many fields – Dylan Thomas, Igor Stravinsky, Graham Sutherland, Léonide Massine, Matisse, Orson Welles and Akira Kurosawa. He was hopeful that each project could have the length it demanded, and thought that perhaps the new medium of television would make this possible. Sadly, he was at least fifteen years ahead of his time.

None of 'Powell's Tales' were ever made, and most remained only projects. But one was extensively developed: an adaptation of 'a Hindu love story' retold by the English writer F. W. Bain in *Descent of the Sun*. It is a legend about two lovers who were doomed to be reborn and not know each other on Earth – but are reunited only when they slay each other. Powell planned it as a dance-drama.

In his 1952 and 1953 diaries he vividly describes his collaboration on the project with Brian Easdale, the resident composer for the Archers after *Black Narcissus* (1947) and *The Red Shoes*; and Hein Heckroth, their resident production designer from *The Red Shoes* on. Loyal Archers collaborators Abraham Sofaer and Esmond Knight were brought in as the project took shape.

Despite little evidence surviving of what it would have been like, Michael's enthusiasm and ability to inspire others come through strongly from his diary entries. It stands as a poignant reminder of the creative energy that all filmmakers devote to projects which never reach the screen.

From the Diaries of Michael Powell

January 4, 1952
I wonder how high I shall jump when I start again after a year of lying fallow. It is over a year since I directed a scene.

January 23, 1952
Dinner with Monique [Tcherina] and Brian [Easdale] & *Descent of the Sun*. We are all inspired. We talk and interrupt each other until 12.00. This is the best film-story in the world.

February 3, 1952
Brian arrived at 11.30 and we set to work (with an interval for lunch) and finished the first draft by 4.0. Brian gets so interested in the Tale that I have to remind him of the music. We phone Hein Heckroth and he comes over with Ada. I read the Tale to him and he sees at once the one weak spot in the narrative: with my back against the wall I have to put it right, and I do.

We three understand one another: director, composer and designer, we create independently in each other's minds. The Tale grows, whether we are alone or together. 'Is the Tale to be direct?' says Hein: meaning is it to be Modern? Neither Brian nor I answer: we are too busy adjusting our own imaginations to this question. Is it Hindu? What is the theme? We all agree that it is the pursuit of the woman by the man, the dream, the raison d'être of every artist, the reason for the existence of Art. What is the title of the Tale? I suggest: 'The Dream'; and give my reasons. Without argument we all start to dream. We often disagree in silence, then make our point clear in action, a painting, a theme of music: and so the Tale grows. How long does Brian need? Six months. Is he to sketch the Themes or write a score? Tomorrow I will dictate the draft. Should the libretto rhyme? Not necessarily. As near to speech as possible.

February 4, 1952

I work with Joan Page [the Archers' long time typist] all the afternoon, dictating the Treatment of *The Descent of the Sun*. I have titled it, for the present, 'The Dream'.

February 5, 1952

All day with Joan Page. Finished at 5.0 as the lights were turned on. The style has changed completely while I am dictating: one of the reasons I hate dictating. Now I shall have to go back over the draft and re-write the first ten pages, at least.

I think it is good. A piece of work which will inspire all my collaborators, and perhaps even explain to a financier or a salesman what it is that makes this story great, and how it can be the best film I have ever made – although not the best I shall ever make: a forerunner of many others, if I am allowed. Tomorrow I shall read it over.

February 7, 1952

I have finished correcting proofs of *Descent of the Sun*, with the new title *The Lotus of the Moon* … I am playing a good deal of Stravinsky. I like his shorter pieces. Surely it is unique to have a Russian artist with a classical mind and an obvious love of the Greeks. I think he would write an extraordinary score for the Odyssey.

February 11, 1952

Life is a dream.

I work on my Tales.

Japan hangs in the air.

America hangs in the air.

I send Monique to Paris to get her visa.

I feel like a squirrel in a cage: or a dreamer who cannot wake.

February 19, 1952

Brian has sent me his thoughts upon the music after reading *The Lotus of the Moon*. I am going over them today, to make my own notes before returning them. He is starting at once upon the themes and the main features of the score. I can feel that this story inspires him as no other has done. Brian's notes take me all day, with minor interruptions. Some of my ideas seem very good but they are chiefly meant to (a) show I have read Brian's (b) irritate and so (c) stimulate.

After Powell's round the world trip in March …

May 15, 1952

I went on to the Pre-Raphaelite house, no. 69 Eton Avenue – where Brian and Noel Lee played me first music for *Lotus of the Moon*. He is inspired and so am I. He played me the Prelude and Postlude: indicated the rhythm of the drumming: and played the first movements of the Lotus Ballet. For the Song of Vanity he has taken the Song of Songs. We go to the Etoile and eat, still talking, still drunk with image + music.

June 23, 1952

I wrestle all day with a little introductory verse to lead into Brian's Prelude to *The Lotus of the Moon*. At last the right lines are written. Now I can get on, even if we never use it.

July 12, 1952

Brian comes to dinner and for a long talk. I read him what I have done on *Lotus of the Moon* and, on the whole, he likes it. He needs it, as he has just got to the same point. I promise to let him have it typed on Tuesday.

December 10, 1952

I go to 69 Eton Avenue to hear the recording of *Lotus of the Moon*, Part One. … The music is good, the recording bad. 'The Lotus Ballet' is wonderful. 'The Song of Solomon' too long. Brian agrees to cut and to give the lovers more of a dance. We can then make 'The Lotus Ballet' one of our Parisian schemes for Monique [Tcherina].

December 22, 1952

I meet Brian at 69 Eton Avenue … we play the stage-version of 'The Lotus Ballet': it runs 33 minutes:

> Prelude
> Variations (the kinds of women)
> The Lotus Born and the Eternal Theme
> The Song of Solomon
> The Lotus Ballet. The Wedding-Procession.
> "Set me as a seal upon thy heart!"

We also went over his scheme for 'Tam o'Shanter' [a proposed episode of *Bouquet*]. The ballet becomes much clearer, as I always knew it would, once the music scheme was reviewed. And for this we must get hold of John Laurie.

February 4, 1953
Brian Easdale arrived, civilized, cultivated, brilliant and lazy. He is ready to start upon the full orchestration of the Lotus Ballet. We all devour Carmen's good dinner and talk until midnight.

October 29, 1953
We recorded the score of *Lotus of the Moon*, up to the point where the lovers fall to earth. It is about 40 minutes of music, speech and narration. Abraham Sofaer spoke Shiva, the Introduction and the Sage. Esmond [Knight] the Englishman on the Bridge and the soliloquy on the two lovers. Jean Lodge, the girl who came to see me the other day, spoke Uma, and an Indian called Sati, the Indian. Brian + a dynamic little woman in yellow enjoyed themselves hugely on two pianos. A slim, intense character in black velvet with a serious, pale, boy's face (I think Cottier is her name) came to listen. She is producing the Ballet at Ballet Workshop on November 15.

Jean Lodge made a great hit with everybody. She has a creamy voice, with a splendid nose and mouth, the kind of haughty, sensual beauty which is seldom seen on our stage. She is a singularly sweet girl, too, with a modest and shy nature behind all the beauty. She is married to Fred O'Shaughnessy, a writer and film-technician who is at the moment producing a film with Finlay Currie [O'Shaughnessy would go on to create *Upstairs Downstairs* for ITV in the 1970s].

I think the recording will need a bit of discreet commentary at key points, to explain the music, e.g. 'the flames mount to heaven', 'The Lotus Ballet', 'The Sage in the Forest' etc. But it is a unique and beautiful way to present a script. Emeric will have none of it and has disowned it. He is a funny old man of the Hampstead mountain.

After the recording we all went to the pub and drank innumerable beers; not really a good idea but it seemed a good idea at the time. We had all enjoyed ourselves so much that we hated to part.

From the unpublished diaries of Michael Powell. (© Thelma Schoonmaker Powell)

Alexander Korda (standing, centre) photographed on set during the production of *The Thief of Bagdad* (1940), with actor June Deprez. (©ITV/BFI National Archive)

2

Exiles

Caitlin McDonald

'There I was with my Hungarian passport, an enemy alien, surrounded by Blimps of all kinds, including the best kind.' – Emeric Pressburger[1]

I t is said that the door of producer Sir Alexander Korda's office bore the pronouncement, 'It's not enough to be Hungarian, you must have talent too.' This may have been a joke at the expense of the new influx of émigré filmmakers, but it was Korda who was to introduce the talented Hungarian Emeric Pressburger to the quintessentially British Michael Powell, setting in motion the process that would join together one of the finest teams of international filmmaking. Korda, like Pressburger, was to leave his home nation as a young adult, and although he arrived in Britain through his own choice in the early 1930s, his Jewish heritage meant that he effectively bore the status of exile after the onset of the Second World War.

Both Korda and Pressburger, two of the most well-known names in British cinema, can be regarded as chameleonic figures who lived transient lifestyles, moving through a number of countries before settling in the United Kingdom. And both altered their Hungarian birth names to adapt to their new nation.[2] Pressburger always regarded himself as Hungarian, but his hometown became part of Romania when he was eighteen, following

---

1. Emeric Pressburger's rough notes for a speech on the making of *49th Parallel*, c. 1978. (BFI National Archive, EPR/1/19/14)
2. Alexander Korda was born as Sándor Kellner, while Pressburger's given name, Imre, was first altered to Emmerich while living in Germany and then anglicised to Emeric after his move to London.

the treaty of Trianon in 1920. This sparked the beginning of his lifelong status as an exile, moving between five nations before his arrival in Britain in 1935. Despite these multi-cultural beginnings, the celebrated director David Lean is said to have commented that, 'Emeric is more English than any of us!'

Michael Powell, on the other hand, had a relatively idyllic childhood in Kent, and other than a brief sojourn in France, stayed in Britain for most of his filmmaking career. Yet he was utterly charmed by European art cinema, theatre and ballet.[3] Listening to Pressburger relay his ideas for *The Spy in Black* (1939), Powell immediately knew he had found his ideal creative collaborator. Over subsequent films they established a working process in which Pressburger developed a script which was then passed back and forth between the two men, being refined in the process. Powell added a director's visual eye, and, especially early on when Pressburger was still learning English, reworked the dialogue. Powell directed but Pressburger was usually on set throughout production making suggestions and overseeing the shoot. Pressburger was also the member of the team who worked most closely with the editor in the cutting room. When they launched the Archers, both acted as producers.

What they both brought to this process was a blending of British sensibilities with Continental influences. It is perhaps this combination that has made their films so enduring, as well as representative of the filmmakers themselves. Powell drew on formative years in the south of France working with Rex Ingram and Harry Lachman at the Metro Studio in Nice. Pressburger brought a sophisticated sensibility to his work but at the same time was able to create a powerful, almost mystical, sense of British place in his scripts. Without this union of talents and lived experiences, and those of their team of collaborators, their films are unlikely to have endured in the public consciousness in quite the same way.

Throughout the 1920s and 30s, filmmakers moved freely between Britain and Continental Europe. This period saw Alfred Hitchcock travelling to studios in Germany for the production of *The Pleasure Garden* (1925) and *The Mountain Eagle* (1926). Others came to Britain from Europe: the Korda brothers, Alexander, Zoltan and Vincent, and the production designer – and key Powell and Pressburger collaborator – Alfred Junge.

---

3. Powell did go on to have a brief period of making films in Australia, making *They're a Weird Mob* (1966) with Pressburger, who wrote it under the pseudonym Richard Imrie, and then *Age of Consent* (1969). This could broadly be regarded as Powell's own exile from the British film industry following a number of poor critical reviews of *Peeping Tom* (1960), which led to him struggling to gain funding within the UK.

Alfred Junge at work on *A Matter of Life and Death* (1946), photographed by Eric Gray. (Eric Gray/© ITV/ BFI National Archive)

Junge started his career in Germany. He worked extensively in the world-leading film industry of his home country throughout the twenties, honing his skills as an art director amongst the great Expressionist sets of the Berlin studios, before travelling to Britain in 1926 to work as an art director as part of E. A. Dupont's team for British International Pictures. By 1932, he had settled permanently in the UK and worked for Gaumont-British. It was during this period in which European, and particularly German, talents were valued in Britain as they brought with them a more lavish *mise-en-scéne* as well as the concept of 'total design', in which key looks for the film were pre-planned on paper to develop the overall mood and emotional register. Junge's influence can be felt from his first work with Powell and Pressburger, as set designer for *Contraband* (1940). In a particularly disorientating sequence, the protagonist hides in a room full of plaster busts of Neville Chamberlain, providing a sense of the uncanny which is lifted straight from German Expressionism. Junge's work on *Black Narcissus* (1947), recreating the Himalayas in Pinewood Studios with sets, model shots and matte paintings won him a well-deserved Academy Award for Art Direction. Junge, like the Korda brothers, could be regarded as a political and economic émigré, who moved to Britain for work but became an exile after

Production design for *Contraband* (1940) by Alfred Junge. (Alfred Junge/© ITV/La Cinémathèque française)

Hitler took control in Germany, which led to a second wave of filmmakers, artists, and writers flocking to her shores.

Like many of the great exiled filmmakers who made new lives in the British film industry and/or Hollywood, Junge launched his film career at the lauded German film studio, Ufa. Most of the talents who would go on to work for the Archers, as well as Pressburger himself, passed through Ufa in the early stages of their film careers, including composer Allan Gray (born in Poland as Josef Zmigrod), cinematographer Erwin Hillier, and actor Conrad Veidt. One of the rare exceptions was Hein Heckroth, who was first celebrated as a designer of theatre, opera and ballet in Germany. He also enjoyed a successful career as a practising artist. The move to cinema only came when he reached the British Isles. Each collaborator made a mark for themselves within the British studio system, but their practice was transformed when they came together in the 1940s under Powell and Pressburger, to produce some of their finest work. One can imagine that having worked as an assistant cameraman on Fritz Lang's *M* (1931) was invaluable preparation for Erwin Hillier, who went on to create the bold chiaroscuro cinematography of *A Canterbury Tale* (1944) and *I Know Where I'm Going!* (1945).

Hein Heckroth at The Arts Theatre, Cambridge, where he was working on a production of *In Wonderland* with fellow exile, Kurt Jooss, 1942. Photographed by Lee Miller. (© Lee Miller/Lee Miller Archive)

Many of the team were to leave Germany after the firing of all Jewish staff from Ufa on 29 March 1933. Pressburger was to flee the country just over a month later, leaving the key in his front door 'to save the Gestapo the trouble of having to break it down.'[4] Most of the exiled filmmakers were to travel to France, forming a brief enclave until some, like Billy Wilder and Peter Lorre, would move onwards to begin careers in Hollywood. Those who would eventually join the Archers travelled on to London.

While having the shared experience of an uprooting from their homes, often fearing for their lives, these exiled filmmakers also had to cope with their ever-growing concern for

---

4. Kevin Macdonald, *Emeric Pressburger: The Life and Death of a Screenwriter* (London: Faber and Faber, 1994), 100.

Emeric Pressburger's Ufa (Universum
Film AG) screening room pass,
Berlin, 1931. (BFI National Archive)

their families left behind. There is a distinction between those who fled because they had
to and were directly under threat from the Nazis as a result of their own Jewish heritage,
such as Pressburger, Gray, and Hillier; and those who left because their wives were Jewish, as well as their own political convictions, such as Heckroth and Veidt. Both would
undoubtedly be unsettling departures, but it is clear that the Jewish refugees would be
left with a deeper and longer lasting trauma. Despite this, Pressburger clearly had great
admiration for those who left for their own convictions and draws attention to this in his
1966 novel, *The Glass Pearls,* wherein a character comments, 'You are not a Jew [...] You
have left for more noble reasons than I wanted to leave for. I was just scared.'[5] It is perhaps
for this reason that Pressburger became good friends with Conrad Veidt, the celebrated

---

5.   Emeric Pressburger, *The Glass Pearls* (London: Faber & Faber, 2015), 28.

Conrad Veidt as Captain Hardt and Valerie Hobson as the School Mistress in *The Spy in Black* (1939). (©ITV/BFI National Archive)

German actor remembered for his role as Cesare the somnambulist in *The Cabinet of Dr Caligari* (Robert Wiene, 1920), who went on to star in Powell and Pressburger's first films together, *The Spy in Black* (1939) and *Contraband* (1940). Veidt was not Jewish, yet he scrawled the word 'Jude' on his exit form as his reason for leaving Germany in 1933, perhaps in solidarity with his wife and Jewish friends.[6] During the early years of the war, Pressburger spent much of his leisure time with the expatriate community of Hungarian and German émigrés, including Veidt. As well as having shared languages, cultures and the experience of being forcibly removed from their homes, the émigré community all bore the label of 'enemy aliens' during the Second World War.

---

6.   Pat Wilks Battle, 'Biography' in *Conrad Veidt on Screen*, ed. by John T. Soister (Jefferson: McFarlane & Co, 2002), 21.

The policy of labelling German, Austrian and Italian nationals came into play in May 1940, but it made little difference if the individual in question was sympathetic to the Nazi party or was a Jewish refugee fleeing from them. As such, Allan Gray and Alfred Junge were interned on the Isle of Man, while Hein Heckroth was interned in Australia. Others, such as Pressburger, were placed under curfew by the Central Registry for Aliens, had belongings such as cameras and radios confiscated, and were required to report to the police once per week. This had a knock-on effect on Pressburger's ability to make films with Powell, in particular, *49th Parallel* (1941), which was filmed in Canada. When Powell and Pressburger toured Canada on a fact-finding mission to scout locations, this was to be the only time they would be able to leave Britain together during the war. During their time in Canada, word came through that France had surrendered. It had a very different impact on each of them, as Powell notes in his autobiography:

> It was one thing for me, who was English, to be so nonchalant about returning to my country in the middle of a disaster, and quite another for Emeric, who was an enemy alien, an artist, a journalist, a writer who had come to England for a haven from Hitler after an uneasy passage through Prague, Berlin and Paris. Yet here he was, planning with me how we should share our divided responsibilities.[7]

This was before Powell and Pressburger would take on the collaborative 'written, produced and directed' credit, but it is clear from Powell's account and the letters between the pair during the production of *49th Parallel* that Pressburger's role was much more involved than a screenwriter's would typically be during the production, and post-production, phase. Although their famous shared credit would not appear until their next film, *One of Our Aircraft is Missing* (1942), they strove for an egalitarian filmmaking partnership. In these circumstances Pressburger's status as an enemy alien hindered the production. Despite being funded by the Ministry of Information as propaganda film, designed ultimately to draw the US into the war, the Home Office blocked Pressburger's ability to join Powell on location in Canada during the film's production, first by conveniently 'losing' his passport, then by declining to grant him permission to return to Britain if he left the country. He writes of his stress in a letter to Powell, where he asks, 'How on earth can I be helpful to you? You must have a very difficult time out there and you certainly think that you are not getting

---

7.   Michael Powell, *A Life in Movies* (London: Faber & Faber, 1986), 353.

Australian poster for *One of Our Aircraft is Missing* (1942). (© Paramount/BFI National Archive)

the support you should from here', before going on to comment that, 'I hope (and am sure) that finally everything will turn out right and we shall have a very great picture. And we shall show to all who begun to doubt in our scheme that they are the idiots and not we.' [8]

This 'enemy alien' label also affected one of the original stars of the film. Elisabeth Bergner was signed up to play the role of the Hutterite, Anna, yet absconded from the production when she reached Canada, seeing it as an opportunity to travel on to Hollywood. Both Bergner and her husband, the director Paul Czinner, were Jewish and had left Europe in order to escape persecution. It may be the case that she wanted to reach the US out of fear that Britain would also fall into Nazi occupation. But in a written account of her relationship to the film she describes what felt like unbearable restrictions placed on her as an enemy alien, particularly as it meant she could not send money to her mother in Italy. She wrote of her annoyance at the British government's treatment of her at the beginning of the war, noting that:

> [W]e had to check in with the police every week, despite the new British citizenship, and a new British passport. Exactly the same as all the new émigrés who had been living in the country for weeks or months. Despite the success, despite the adoration, in spite of everything. I was speechless. Outraged. I was deeply offended.[9]

Seeing North America as a land of potentially more freedoms, along with the possibility of being reunited with friends, Bergner refused to return to London to shoot interior shots and was replaced by Glynis Johns. Her account of having to register with the police is indicative of the feelings shared by fellow exiles living in the UK, even though it appears she had it easy in comparison to those who faced internment.

49th Parallel follows a group of Nazis journeying across Canada to reach the US border, encountering a host of diverse Canadians along the way. The film is a rare example of British wartime propaganda that also represents Nazi Germany as individualised, varied and nuanced. Lieutenant Hirth, in a powerful performance by Eric Portman, represents the most fanatical Nazi follower who will stop at nothing for their cause. On the other

---

8. Letter from Emeric Pressburger in London to Michael Powell in Canada, 7 September 1940. (BFI National Archive, EPR/1/19/7).

9. Translation of an account by Elizabeth Bergner of her part in *49th Parallel*. No date. (BFI National Archive, EPR-1–19–17).

hand, Vogel, played by Niall MacGinnis, is an atypical film character of the period: a kind-hearted German Nazi. This is one of the first examples of Powell and Pressburger depicting the 'enemy' as sympathetic and, more importantly, human. Vogel notes that he was led, as many Germans were, to join the Party as, 'when you are a boy you like playing soldiers, when you are a young man you can't get work unless you belong to them, when you are an old man you are anxious not to lose what you've got.' This was a controversial piece of dialogue at a time when Nazis were largely depicted as inhuman monsters.

But perhaps the most interesting character in the film is Peter the Hutterite, played by Anton Walbrook. Walbrook, born in Austria as Adolf Wohlbrück, found fame as a romantic lead in several German films, before being forced to emigrate in 1936. As a homosexual of Jewish descent, Walbrook was acutely aware of what it was to live in fear of the spread of Nazism: a fear that he channelled into his performances. *49th Parallel* was the first of four films that Walbrook would make with Powell and Pressburger. By all appearances, Powell and Pressburger would have continued their partnership with Conrad Veidt following the success of *The Spy in Black* and *Contraband*. But Veidt's relocation to Hollywood in 1940, followed by his untimely death in 1943, meant that they turned to Walbrook to

Anton Walbrook, photographed in character as Boris Lermontov for *The Red Shoes* (1948), by George Cannons. (George Cannons/© ITV/ BFI National Archive)

take on board the role of sympathetic foreigner in their later productions. Walbrook, with his softer Viennese accent, brought an element of continental charm to these roles, while Veidt, with his sharp features and strong Berliner accent was sadly typecast as a German Nazi for the rest of his acting career. Walbrook was perfectly cast as Peter, the leader of a religious group who fled from Germany to Canada to farm the land and live free from persecution. The film pivots on a speech in which Peter, who has until that point remained calm and welcoming to his guests, realises that his guests are in fact German Nazis, and makes a passionate argument against the prevailing Hitler-led rhetoric of evil. He makes it clear that despite their shared nationality, they do not share a philosophy:

> You think we hate you, but we don't. It is against our faith to hate. We only hate the power of evil which is spreading across the world. You and your Hitlerism are like the microbes of some filthy disease, filled with a longing to multiply yourselves, until you destroy everything healthy in the world. No, we are not your brothers.

The speech underscores the importance of having both a screenwriter and a performer who had witnessed first-hand the malevolence of Hitlerism, and who were both dismayed by what it was doing to their homelands. While these potent words would still have weight and meaning in the hands of another actor, Walbrook's personal experiences offer greater significance and depth. It's an emotional resonance that can be felt through Walbrook's roles, none more so than in the character of Theo Kretschmar-Schuldorff in *The Life and Death of Colonel Blimp* (1943). Theo represents those Germans who had worked hard all their lives, fought in the Great War, yet would not support the Nazi cause, even if it meant losing contact with children and loved ones who would become followers of the party in 1940s Germany. Theo's speech to the judge of the Alien Tribunal, wherein he claims that he was homesick for England, the home of his late wife, is one of the most moving and persuasive anti-Nazi speeches in British cinema. It highlights the destructive power of Nazism on the lives of everyday Germans, even if they were not Jewish. As the film progresses and the viewer grows attached to Theo, his embittered 'Heil Hitler' – after he recalls that neither of his sons came to his wife's funeral – seems even more powerful.

Theo is often regarded as the most significant and complex exilic character in Powell and Pressburger's filmography, yet all of Walbrook's roles for the duo shared some traits in common with exiles. The exhilarating yet uncompromising ballet impresario, Boris Lermontov of *The Red Shoes*, may not be an exile in name; but the Russian is certainly comfortable with his transient lifestyle, and shows no evidence of having ties with his homeland. Lermontov

Poster for the Japanese release of *The Life and Death of Colonel Blimp* (1943, poster undated). (BFI National Archive)

has been likened by many to Powell, as well as founder of the Ballets Russes, Sergei Diaghilev. But there is more than a hint of the migratory storyteller Pressburger, who liked to weave autobiographical details into the characters that he created. Similarly, Dr Falke or 'the Bat' in Powell and Pressburger's reimagining of *Die Fledermaus*, the post-war set *Oh... Rosalinda!!*, does not sit comfortably within his home society of Vienna. Instead, he flits freely between the occupying nations, adapting to each one with the ease of Walbrook or Pressburger himself.

Looking at Pressburger's canon as a whole, it is clear that the dislocation he experienced from his home nation of Hungary and his adopted home nation of Germany, was to have a lasting effect on his characters. Within all of his films, novels, and screenplays there are examples of characters that do not sit easily within the culture that they find themselves in.

There are obvious cases throughout *Blimp*. But the spirit of something out of time or out of place is omnipresent. Joan Webster (Wendy Hiller), is a middle-class Englishwoman who has to adapt to fit within the remote Scottish community in *I Know Where I'm Going!*; the soldiers and land girl of *A Canterbury Tale*, stationed in rural Kentish Chillingbourne, are also placed out of their depth, as are the Anglican nuns of *Black Narcissus*. This adaptation of Rumer Godden's novel was suggested by Powell, but it is Pressburger's own experiences that colour the screenplay's increasingly unbridled tension between the land, the culture and its inhabitants.

The detachment from one's home or place of comfort is also evident in the two novels that Pressburger was to publish in the 1960s. His first, *Killing a Mouse on Sunday* (1960), is the story of Manuel Artiguez, a Spanish Republican exiled in France after the Civil War, who is lured back to his home by a Guardia Civil using Artiguez's dying mother as a trap. There are parallels between this and Pressburger's desire to bring his own mother from Hungary to Britain during the war. Tragically, like so many others, she was killed in a concentration camp, and Pressburger is said to have felt guilt for this for the rest of his life.

Pressburger's second novel, *The Glass Pearls* (1966), took the character of the exiled 'good German' to the extreme. The main character, Karl Braun, is a German Nazi living in hiding in London after the war, at the time of the Nuremberg trials for Nazi war criminals. He appears mild-mannered and friendly to those around him, but Pressburger gradually reveals that he bears the weight of some of the worst crimes against humanity. Perhaps even more surprising is that Pressburger used some of his own experiences within the narrative, and that Herr Braun, consumed by fear and living far from home, shares more than a passing resemblance to his creator and other key Pressburger-like characters. Both Braun and Pressburger emit the cosmopolitan sophistication of Lermontov; the loss and longing for their home of Theo; and Joan's overriding sense of being an outsider. This late work, as well as his unpublished novels (now cared for by the BFI National Archive), reveal the lasting trauma that the Holocaust and his exiled status had on his personal and professional life.

It is assumed that many exiles return home as soon as it is safe to do so, but many of those who worked with the Archers now had strong ties to the nation that had provided shelter in the darkest period of their life. Alfred Junge, Erwin Hillier and Allan Gray all established long careers in Britain after the war. Hein Heckroth stayed in Britain for nearly a decade before returning to work in Germany, continuing his experimental approach across the performing and screen arts (including Powell's televised version of Bartók's *Bluebeard's Castle*, made for Süddeutscher Rundfunk in 1963).

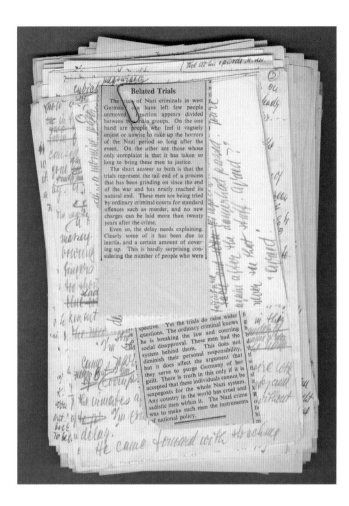

Emeric Pressburger's handwritten notes and research cuttings for *The Glass Pearls*, 1966. (© Emeric Pressburger/BFI National Archive)

Anton Walbrook, who, in his British work away from the Archers was too often type-cast as a mysterious and manipulating yet sexually alluring foreigner, made films in the UK as well as France, but was to spend his latter career working in West German television. Despite passing away in Bavaria, Walbrook's remains were interred in London as he had wished, demonstrating the strength of his feelings towards his adopted homeland. Pressburger remained in Britain other than a brief move to the Austrian Tyrol in the 1970s. He returned to Britain after experiencing anti-Semitism, once again forced from his home because of persecution. He spent the rest of his life living in a quiet village in Suffolk; a peaceful and stable existence after a turbulent life. He continued to write until the end of his life and although most of the later works remain incomplete, they show how the screenwriter who became a British citizen and deeply immersed himself in British life was to always retain the hybrid identity of the exile.

Right: Michael Powell and Emeric Pressburger during the production of *A Canterbury Tale* (1944), photographed by Felix H. Man (Hans Felix Sigismund Baumann). Man specialised in what he termed 'reportage portraits'. 'I had no sittings' he says, just 'photo-interviews'. 'Thus the method I used in portraying people was based on precisely the same principles I had developed as a photo-journalist: "writing with the camera instead of the pen" and leaving everything undisturbed.' (Felix H Man/© ITV/ BFI National Archive)

Left: Pamela Brown, photographed at Vogue Studios, London, 1942, by Lee Miller. Miller, a leading figure in photography and the arts, was Head of British *Vogue* Studio in these years, as well as working as a war photographer and correspondent in Continental Europe. (© Lee Miller/Lee Miller Archive)

The darkness and disorientation of the blackout conveyed in production designs for (above) *A Canterbury Tale* (1944) by Alfred Junge; and (below) *The Small Back Room* (1949) by Ivor Beddoes. (Alfred Junge/© ITV/The Harry Ransom Center; Ivor Beddoes/© STUDIOCANAL/ BFI National Archive)

Hein Heckroth's designs for *The Tales of Hoffmann* (1951) are full of his memories of dislocation. They are other-worldly, drawing on his surrealist imagination and his personal reflections on war. This design for Giulietta (top), stepping over the bodies of her victims, is one such sombre but beautiful artwork. (Hein Heckroth/©ITV/BFI National Archive)

Notes from a Photographer

Tim Walker

Like many, I first watched Powell and Pressburger at home on a Sunday afternoon. It planted a set of feelings that I have returned to again and again. Much of my work as a photographer has been about stepping into these moments of my childhood. I might revisit the mood of a film in a myriad of ways, taking the essence without recreating it.

In *A Matter of Life and Death* (1946), when June falls in love with just a voice, it's one of those extraordinary moments in cinema. So many writers, artists and filmmakers have dabbled in the theme of the emotional female falling in love, but Powell and Pressburger truly mastered it. As the camera lingers on the close up of June – falling in love with a man that she has only heard, never seen – the capacity for romance feels endless. It creates the astonishing possibility of *something* in an otherwise desperate moment.

I'm ultimately drawn to the surfaces on characters, and June's lipstick has stayed with me. Seen in extreme close up, with its cakey texture, there's a softness and beauty in the cinematography by Jack Cardiff. I've photographed mostly women to date, and I've always been struck by the art of lighting a person's skin and make-up. I often think of this scene as I see make-up being applied for a shoot. But more than any other character, Conductor 71 (Marius Goring) stays in my mind: an Englishman's perception of the French, set against the deep fuchsia of the rhododendron bush. Romantic and exotic, he is extraordinary in so many ways. Yet his words ring with tenderness and truth. It's these contrasts that we crave and that give depth to each detail.

I admire the fact that Powell and Pressburger were not afraid to embrace the whole-heartedly artificial. As a photographer this resonates with me. My work is intensely

June (Kim Hunter) amongst the rhododendron bushes in *A Matter of Life and Death* (1946), photographed by Eric Gray. (Eric Gray/© ITV/BFI National Archive)

Stella Tennant and pink powder cloud, Englingham Hall, Northumberland, 2007, photographed by Tim Walker.
(© Tim Walker/Collection of the artist)

Lily Donaldson and the blue Spitfire, Glenham Hall, Suffolk, March 2009. (© Tim Walker/Collection of the artist)

artificial, yet within the artifice you're looking for someone to do something that's true. A gesture or a chink in the armour that reveals the human condition. We continually seek out organic shapes, feelings and textures that remind us of our shared humanity. Quite often this can be nature itself, or it might be a moment of pure serendipity. There's a real joy to be found in the accidental. I like to think that within the regimented world of film production – where scenes might be storyboarded, scripted and lit to happen in a certain way – there was an openness to the way in which Powell and Pressburger worked. They had the ability to go to where the beauty and humanity was, not to just follow the action. Perhaps that came from who they worked with.

The cinematography throughout is beautiful. It gives many of the films their distinctive lustre. *Black Narcissus* leaves me with the feeling of ice-like straight lines and blocky, chunky shapes. In *The Red Shoes*, there's an overstated use of gels on camera; like a sweet wrapper held up to the light, just to see what it does.

Production design for the opening scenes of *A Matter of Life and Death* (1946) by Alfred Junge. (Alfred Junge/
©ITV/The Harry Ransom Center)

3

Pilgrims

Alexandra Harris

As his stricken Lancaster Bomber roars to an infernal blaze in *A Matter of Life and Death* (1946), Peter Carter strengthens himself with a few last lines of poetry. 'Give me my scallop-shell of quiet', he yells into the din. The words are from 'The Passionate Man's Pilgrimage', thought to have been written by Walter Raleigh as he awaited execution.[1] Then a snatch of Andrew Marvell ('what a marvel') urging his coy mistress to seize the moment since earthly time is short and deserts lie beyond. These are Peter's literary last rites, allowing him to link arms across centuries with writers who are his heroes, his friends, his chosen guides to this world and the next. He is embarking on a more extended and more passionate pilgrimage than he yet knows: one that will take him through the cosmos to heaven, and back again to life and love.

The Archers and their collaborators of the 1940s might justifiably have pinned the scallop-shell, the ancient pilgrim's token, to their coats. Again and again, they reimagined what pilgrimage might be in modern times. They asked what was worth seeking, and how it could be found, what draws different kinds of people together on the road, what unexpected shrines might take on mystical significance. In *A Canterbury Tale* (1944) they offered a sequel to Chaucer's gallimaufry of wayside stories, so that Bob from Oregon and the shop-girl Alison take their places on the Old Pilgrims' Way with the Knight and the Wife of Bath, adding their

---

1. Attributed to Walter Raleigh, 'The Passionate Man's Pilgrimage', line 1, *The Poems of Sir Walter Ralegh: A Historical Edition*, ed. Michael Rudick (Tempe: Arizona Center for Medieval and Renaissance Studies, 1999), 126.

voices to the human chorus. Then, while waiting to film *A Matter of Life and Death*, which is the story of a traveller mislaid, they diverted their energies into the Hebridean voyage of *I Know Where I'm Going!* which is itself a journey paused, sent off course, and reconsidered.

As he began work on *A Canterbury Tale* in 1943, Michael Powell was homeward bound, returning to the Kentish fields and villages of his childhood. His father had been a farmer, largely a hop-grower, in the village of Bekesbourne just outside Canterbury; young Michael and his brother grew up – through the years of the First World War – among hop poles, oasts, and orchards. The film goes with Powell back into that childhood, stooping to catch the vantage point of boys as they engage in elaborate mock-battles on the banks of the Stour. Inviting crew and country to his native place, Powell was the host, or (to use a word he liked) the 'conductor' showing the way. Yet Pressburger, separated forever from his own childhood places in Hungary, also felt a strong personal attachment to the film. Of all the Archers' productions, this was the one he considered his own.[2] It's a striking reversal of expectation but characteristic of the Archers' partnership, in which distinctive, unpredictable, inexhaustible cinema comes from the collaborative merging of viewpoints.

Before they turned to Chaucer, there was talk of a film based on John Bunyan's *The Pilgrim's Progress*. Their backer J. Arthur Rank was a Methodist, interested in the possibilities of religious film, and keen on the idea. Pressburger, meanwhile, was understandably doubtful. Though all his scripts have a strong feeling for allegory, they also work through idiosyncratic personal encounters, accidents, interruptions, particularities of time and place; and they resist any directly Christian interpretation. Bunyan would remain an influential figure for the Archers; indeed Powell liked to think he would eventually be escorted to heaven by Bunyan and Kipling together.[3] But for now, Pressburger resolved to write a new pilgrimage story and chose Chaucer to begin it.

Pressburger reached for the materials of his story: an ancient road, a village, medieval voices sounding in the grass. In *A Canterbury Tale* he raised acute questions about tradition and belonging. He was necessarily asking what English landscape meant to him,

---

2. Pressburger said, 'this is the only one of them that is entirely mine'. Kevin Macdonald, *Emeric Pressburger, The Life and Death of a Screenwriter* (London: Faber and Faber, 1994), 234.

3. Bunyan's significance for the Archers is examined in revelatory detail by the Bunyan scholar Michael Davies. See 'The Relevant Pilgrim: John Bunyan in A Matter of Life and Death', in W.R. Owens and Stuart Sim (eds), *Reception, Appropriation, Recollection: Bunyan's Pilgrim's Progress* (Bern, Switzerland: Peter Lang, 2007), 185–211.

Sheila Sim as Alison Smith in *A Canterbury Tale* (1944) photographed by Fred Daniels. Daniels was a regular Archers collaborator between 1941 and 1955 as both still and portrait photographer. (Fred Daniels/©ITV/ BFI National Archive)

what all these affirmations of English history had to offer in modern times, what feelings of possession or detachment they might arouse. Peter Conrad articulates part of what is most powerful in the film when he describes it as 'an act of continuation that is also a meditation on continuity'.[4]

As an 'enemy alien' in England, Pressburger was denied permission to stay overnight in Kent – even though he was making a film with patriotic aims for the enhancement of Anglo-American relations. If he was frustrated, it did not show in a script that takes full and loving possession of green verges and hill-tops. Other key crew members were allowed into

---

4.   Peter Conrad, *To Be Continued: Four Stories and their Survival* (Oxford University Press, 1995), 24.

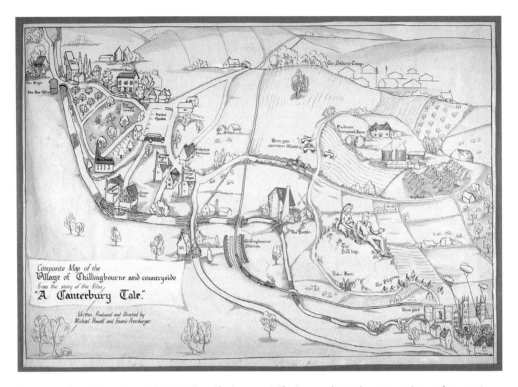

Map design for *A Canterbury Tale* (1944) by Alfred Junge. (Alfred Junge/© ITV/La Cinémathèque française)

the garden of England though they too were far from Kentish. Allan Gray (Józef Żmigrod), who came from Austrian Galicia and had studied with Schönberg, gave Chillingbourne its soundtrack and composed the extraordinary Canterbury montage of pealing bells and 'Onward Christian Soldiers'.[5] The young Erwin Hillier, German Jewish and trained in Berlin, masterminded the immersive photography, long sequences of which reawaken for cinema the history of British landscape art. He puts the camera low to the ground, down in the long grass where perhaps the echo of medieval hooves is still audible. But he also follows the upward glance of characters who snuff the air for something beyond themselves; he catches the daylight in their eyes, and the energy of the moving sky they inhabit.[6]

5. On Gray's work with the Archers see: K. J. Donnelly, 'I Know Where I'm Going!: Hearing Germanic Music in the Scottish Isles', in Tim Bergfelder and Christian Cargnelli (eds), *Destination London: German-Speaking Emigrés and British Theatre, 1925–50* (New York: Berghahn Books, 2008), 220–30.

6. Powell remembered Hillier being, if anything, a little too attentive to the weather. He was 'loony' about clouds and 'detested a clear sky'. Michael Powell, *A Life in Movies* (London: Faber & Faber, 1986), 443.

The sets – from village wheelwright to olde oaken inns – were the responsibility of Alfred Junge. Like Hillier he retained a strong taste for the arts of his native Germany; often, from a deep-shadowed scene, some mysterious aspect of English life will emerge. He had a way of infusing the metaphysical or sublime with playfulness, and a genius for mixing exuberant symbolism with local detail. Starting work on *A Canterbury Tale* he sat down with long reading lists in Kensington library, studied the Ellesmere manuscript in facsimile, drew out diagrams of how each pilgrim's horse should be appropriately harnessed to reflect character and social status.[7] There was a valuing of historical research here of which even Nikolaus Pevsner might have approved.

Like Chaucer's pilgrims and their wartime counterparts, the film crew was a travelling group, telling stories together, bringing their individual perspectives. Their film was about just that: people with differing pasts and visions brought together in a common quest. Alison has come to Kent to work with the Land Army; Peter Gibbs is joining his army unit; and the American GI Bob Johnson (played by a US army sergeant) is trying to visit Canterbury, having promised his mother he'd see the cathedral, but gets off the train at Chillingbourne by mistake, unable to see the signs in the black-out. The Archers specialised in such botched arrivals; we know there'll be a long delay before Bob gets to where he was going. Like a knight-errant in the forests of romance, he stumbles on adventure. So they are all here more or less by chance: three pilgrims as un-Kentish as the Cook, and the Reeve and Alysson the Wife of Bath.

A Canterbury Tale belongs to a time when the celebration of deep England was, for many, a solace, motivation, and survival strategy. Villages were invoked, with passionate conviction on the part of urban and country people alike, as the shorthand answer to the great question 'what are we fighting for?' In the *English Villages* volume of 'Britain in Pictures' (a whole series of popular books devoted to aspects of national culture), Edmund Blunden offered, in opposition to warfare, the 'beautiful and purposeful' work of apple gatherers in the Kent village of his own childhood.[8] The title of C. Henry Warren's 1941 book *England is a Village* summed up its argument that the nation's best qualities are found in the rhythmic, organised life of the rural community, where the lambing carried on despite bombers flying overhead.[9] Continuity was always the watchword. If histories of

---

7. For his preparatory notes and drawings see: A Canterbury Tale, Box 8, Folder 9, Alfred Junge Collection, Harry Ransom Centre, The University of Texas at Austin, USA. Accessed 19 Jan. 2021. https://hrc.contentdm.oclc.org/digital/collection/p15878coll33/id/1655

8. Edmund Blunden, *English Villages* (London: William Collins, 1942), 18.

9. Clarence Henry Warren, *England is a Village* (London: Eyre and Spottiswode, 1941).

change and violence were mentioned – riots, poverty, religious persecution, civil war – it was to show how villages absorbed such shocks and endured.

The Archers did not hold back. *A Canterbury Tale* proffers a feast of beloved village features, touring the square with its lop-sided cottages, the forge and the wheelwright's shop, the church, village hall, and ancient inn; a laden haywain rolls by. Junge wanted the details just right. John Britton's antiquarian surveys of Kent were not available at the public library during the war, but there was plenty left, including *Old Inns of Kent* (1925) and Arthur Oswald's study of local country houses.[10] Junge saw how the stuff of Batsford guides and antiquarian gazetteers might shade readily into gothic, and he conjured Expressionist shadows to provoke a gentle shiver at Chillingbourne's inn The Hand of Glory. The obligatory carved four-poster bed (complete with story of Queen Elizabeth's visit) becomes a dark theatre nearly enveloping its sweet American visitor in his pyjamas. 'Hands of glory' were mummified hands kept as relics – liable to look particularly freakish when displayed for adoration. There's no talk of saints' limbs in modern Chillingbourne but the inn sign hangs over the action, pointing a sinister finger – or offering a shake of the hand.

The film draws attention to village features less often noted in the guidebooks: habits of judgemental dismissiveness and defensive superiority. Bob the American, with his 'upside-down' sergeant's stripes, is assumed to be clueless and ready to tote his gun like a gangster ('this is Chillingbourne not Chicago!'). Alison is watched keenly by local labourers as she manoeuvres her cart-horse; they can't wait for the Londoner to make a fool of herself. In fact she is thoroughly capable and longs for a rural life. She also knows and cares about the old road as much as anyone, including the preacher of history, the peculiar predatory Puck and vision-conjuring Prospero, the magus, magistrate and madman, Mr Colpeper.

If the film is a modern morality play, as Powell indicated, it's difficult to know where to place Colpeper in its scheme.[11] His misogyny is such that he happily keeps a ducking-stool above his desk and explains that it was 'very sensibly used for silencing talkative women'. Shocks like this rumble through the film and make their point: there are dangers in wholesale worship of the past; not all its relics are fit to become our shrines. Colpeper's lantern lectures are a kind of enchantment (he casts his shadow in the circle of lamplight like a wolf howling to the moon) but his magic is both black and white. He must learn that the individual lives and insights of Chillingbourne's contemporary visitors, even the women, matter as

---

10. A Canterbury Tale, Box 8, Folder 9, Alfred Junge Collection, Harry Ransom Centre, University of Texas at Austin. D.C. Maynard, *Old Inns of Kent* (London: Philip Allan & Co, 1925); Arthur Oswald, *Country Houses of Kent* (London: Country Life, 1933).

11. Powell, *A Life in Movies*, 447.

much as the pilgrims of centuries past. But he is right that they continue each other. 'They sweated and paused for breath just as you did today', he says, rapt, as if breathing with them.

Chaucer doesn't seem to have been fussed about getting his pilgrims to Canterbury; he left off his book and left them all still on the road, walking and storytelling without end. Powell and Pressburger take their travellers onwards to the cathedral. Alison's hallowed place is less the soaring vaults than a caravan dustily stored at a garage across town, precious reminder of a perfect holiday spent with her fiancé before he went to war. For Peter, the moment of arrival comes when he sits at the cathedral organ after years plying his trade on cinema Wurlitzers; as he begins Bach's *Toccata and Fugue in D Minor*, the divergent worlds of cinema and cathedral are united. In fact, much of the bombed church was cordoned off, the stained glass removed, the great windows boarded up, and the organ dismantled for the duration; but with the alchemy of Hillier's camera, the strenuous work of Alfred Junge in building an entire reconstruction at Denham studios and the sound artistry of Allan Gray, the Archers re-opened the cathedral, restored the organ, and let the bells ring out.[12]

The arrival of people in new places, mostly by accident, is one of the Archers' great and recurring subjects. *I Know Where I'm Going!* studies the responses of the strong-willed Joan who comes to the Hebrides and glances around her with indifference before impatiently powdering her nose. But she can't fail to notice that there are mountains rising through mist across the water.

Pressburger told Powell that he had long wanted to make a film 'about a girl who wants to get to an island'. 'A storm stops her getting there and by the time the storm has died down she no longer wants to go there, because her life has changed quite suddenly in the way girls' lives do'.[13] It was the change that interested him. Joan, the woman he invented, has been charging through life since she learned to crawl, her eyes set on one goal after the next. The main action sees her travelling to the imagined Isle of Kiloran, where she is to marry an older, wealthy industrialist who is sitting out the war on a Scottish island rented from the Laird (Roger Livesey). Everything is just-so: her face composed, her future finances assured, and the sleeper train is an arrow shooting towards her scheduled destination. But in the Archers' target-practice logo, most arrows land a little wide of the mark.

---

12. Photographs of the interior of Canterbury Cathedral were scaled up to huge size, while the bells were models rung by expert bell ringers.

13. Quoted in Macdonald, *Emeric Pressburger*, 242.

The 2021 BFI restoration of *I Know Where I'm Going!* (1945), showing part of Joan Webster's (Wendy Hiller) dream sequence as she starts her journey to Kiloran. (Restored by the BFI National Archive and The Film Foundation in association with ITV. Restoration funding provided by the Hobson/Lucas Family Foundation. Additional support provided by Matt Spick). (©ITV/BFI National Archive)

Delayed on Mull by the weather, Joan falls in love with the real owner of Kiloran, who can't afford to live there and rents it out. Strenuously resisting and then at last giving herself into Torquil's hands, Joan undergoes a moral conversion. As she wavers from her course, she starts to notice the world around her. She acknowledges that there may be things of worth beyond her current sum of knowledge. 'Kindness rules the world, not money', said Pressburger in the summer of 1944, as Powell responded, visibly moved, to a first reading of the script.[14] The story was a moral fable: a choice between the representatives of one life and another.

---

14. Powell, *A Life in Movies*, 468.

Powell was 'bewitched by the magic' of Colonsay (which became Kiloran) on his first visit there during the location-hunting reconnaissance of early summer 1944, and relished his time on Mull, marking up maps, exploring abandoned castles, rock-climbing, taking notes from field guides and folklore records, and keeping *The West Coast Pilot* to hand because an island film-maker must pay attention to the sea as much as dry ground.[15] He found in these islands the antidote to the goal-oriented materialism represented by Joan's intended husband. Here was community; here was partnership with nature and hard, practical, hands-on work; here was natural grandeur and human modesty; here was kindness, and a great deal of joy. All this must somehow be embodied by Torquil, and made palpable in the landscape photography.

Perversely, optimistically, the Archers cast as Torquil an actor who could not come and film in the Hebrides. Roger Livesey was committed to a London play, and missed the whole

Joan (Wendy Hillier) arrives on the Isle of Mull in *I Know Where I'm Going!* (1945). Photographed by Max Rosher. (Max Rosher/© ITV/BFI National Archive)

---

15. Powell, *A Life in Movies*, 461–6.

location shoot. So, in a feat of logistical conjuring and technical brilliance that exceeded even the recreation of Canterbury Cathedral, studio footage of Livesey was stitched together with Scottish scenes featuring a double. As if in compensation for the hero's absence, Powell went to extreme lengths to put himself – and Erwin Hillier with the camera – in the midst of storm, and fog, and waterfall. Greedy for the elements, he immersed himself on behalf of every film-viewer who couldn't get to the winds and waters of the Western Isles.

This was not 'his' landscape in any way – not like Kent, or North Devon. It was thrillingly new, and all the more appreciated after years of wartime restriction on travel: 'as if we were visiting a foreign country after being penned down for years'.[16] But Powell had spent intense months filming *The Edge of the World* on Foula in summer 1936 and *The Spy in Black* in the Orkneys in 1939. In the Hebrides he felt a strong sense of recognition. The islands were strange and familiar at once, and the film would inhabit both viewpoints. Like *A Canterbury Tale* it's a film of tension and attraction between outsiders and insiders, between travellers and hosts. The newcomers are sometimes at odds with the rhythms of the place and disrespectful of tides. But it's the newcomers who help to unlock the rusted-up secrets of the land.

Joan didn't mean to be so diverted on the way to Kiloran. Nor does Peter Carter in *A Matter of Life and Death* expect a sudden romance on his way to the afterlife. The film follows the airman and would-be poet as he miraculously survives when he bails out of his damaged plane without a parachute. The registrars wait for him anxiously in heaven while the cosmic clock ticks on. The delay flouts the laws of the universe, where the records of life and death are printed in triplicate, stamped and filed. There's as much bureaucracy in heaven as in the Ministry of Information offices at Senate House and aberrant statistics are extremely inconvenient. But as Peter will vigorously protest, it's hardly his fault. Unclaimed by death (the conductor having missed him due to low visibility in English fog), Peter falls from his plane into the sea, wakes up, bobs about gently, and comes ashore. It's a classic scene of rebirth. Peter is a re-gendered Venus stepping from the sea; he is Viola washed up after shipwreck in *Twelfth Night* who can but ask in bafflement, 'What country, friends, is this?'[17]

---

16. Powell, *A Life in Movies*, 461.

17. Shakespeare, *Twelfth Night*, 1:2.

Costume design for airman Peter Carter (David Niven) in *A Matter of Life and Death* (1946) by Hein Heckroth.
(Hein Heckroth/© ITV/BFI National Archive)

It's very like Greek Arcadia: there's even a piping goatherd on the sand. This is paradise according to a reader of classical and Renaissance poetry. Theocritus and Virgil and Spenser would be at home. It's also the afterlife imagined by Marvell: 'And yonder all before us lie / Deserts of vast eternity.'[18] Peter fell from the plane with those words in his mind, and here he is on desert sand. But there's a beautiful American woman on a bicycle coming towards him. The place turns out to be England: an English beach out of bounds in wartime, disorientatingly empty, lit like a dream. By the time the Next World realises its mistake, Peter has fallen in love.

Canterbury and Mull had been geographically particular settings, each with a definite weave of history, community, weather, light, topography. The Shropshire of *Gone to Earth* (1950) would be locally distinct again, the camera drawn to what makes it unique; no-one could mistake the jagged silhouette of the Stiperstones for anywhere else. But all these are archetypal places too: cathedral city, island ('a woman goes to an island'), Celtic border country. For *A Matter of Life and Death*, Powell knew that they needed somewhere beautiful, magical even, but without local distinction – which is a strange thing to ask of a place.

Heading out on excursions from his North Devon house, he found what he sought in the dunes and open beaches of Saunton Sands. 'There was a light haze over the landscape, making luminous colour on the cliffs and a flat milky sheet over the sea'.[19] This coast, he thought, looked like Corfu; but then again 'it could have been any country, here or hereafter' – and so it is in Jack Cardiff's photography: international arcadia and Devon seaside. A rhododendron glade adds a tropical-looking twist, lush and lurid in its enhanced Technicolor pinks and greens, but this is perfectly credible flora for ericaceous English soil.

If this is earth, what is heaven? Though Peter's official conductor (Conductor 71), a French aristocrat from the full-costume pageant of history's dead, has come to show the way, he has many other guides and Raleigh not least among them. As so often in the Archers' films, a fleeting allusion unfurls a whole pattern of correspondences. Peter inherits and re-routes the Elizabethan poet's pilgrimage as surely as Chillingbourne's wartime visitors continued the journey of Chaucer's travellers. Raleigh had made his share of epic voyages (and his name was aptly invoked in a film about Anglo-American connection), but in 1604 he prepared for the greater journey into the afterlife. He, or at least the author of the poem, for the attribution has been much questioned since the 1940s, imagined that his

---

18. Andrew Marvell, 'To His Coy Mistress', lines 23–4, in *The Complete Poems*, ed. Elizabeth Story Donnon (London: Penguin, 2005), 50.

19. Quoted in Macdonald, *Emeric Pressburger*, 242.

Jennifer Jones as Hazel Woodus in *Gone to Earth* (1950), photographed by Bert Cann. (Bert Cann/© Disney/ BFI National Archive)

soul, 'like a white palmer', would travel to heaven. There would be no return, no carrying back of palm leaves as souvenir. In the poem, he imagines filling his traveller's water-bottle at paradisal fountains, following holy paths set with rubies.[20]

Alfred Junge was not going to show holy paths set with rubies. He sketched – and built in the studio – a modernist afterlife with aesthetics more reminiscent of a space ship or aerodrome or Tecton's penguin pool for London Zoo. Imagery from the Bible and other holy books was coolly neutralised in a non-denominational heaven where posthumous airmen register at the gleaming check-in desk, and take receipt of standard-issue wings. Raleigh anticipated 'nectar fountains' and the kiss with which he would touch his lips to the bowl of bliss. Pilgrims in *A Matter of Life and Death* must make do with a vending machine by the lockers, and are pleased enough with a Coca-Cola.

They pass into a cosmically scaled amphitheatre. Is this what, in 'The Passionate Man's Pilgrimage', is called 'heaven's bribeless hall'? Raleigh was falsely charged on earth and put his faith in the higher justice of God's court. 'For there Christ is the king's attorney / Who pleads for all without degrees / And he hath angels, but no fees'. Peter Carter, lacking Christ, spends a long time looking for an attorney, and finds the answer is a friend and doctor whose death, indirectly, gives Peter life. Raleigh anticipated a 'grand twelve million jury'; as Hillier's camera pans the Archers' afterlife, which looks, as Christie says, like a United Nations council, we see an extraordinary merging of Renaissance vision with a future of systematically debated international justice.[21]

There is calm music in the spheres of this clockwork universe. The angel-wings are clean, uniforms ironed, everyone seated according to their profession or army division. It's characteristically wry of the Archers to make heaven look magnificent yet dull. Time to resume life's pilgrimage on earth. Raleigh won a last-minute reprieve and lived – though mostly in confinement – for another fifteen years; Peter wins his case against death and is allowed to live happily with June – if not ever-after, then at least for a generous span until he must start this strange journey again.

20. Raleigh, 'Pilgrimage', lines 31–34, in *Poems*, ed. Rudick, 127.
21. Ian Christie, *A Matter of Life and Death* (London: British Film Institute, 2000), 36.

Unrealised production design for the transition between Earth and the Other World in *A Matter of Life and Death* (1946) by Hein Heckroth. (Hein Heckroth/© ITV/BFI National Archive)

Unrealised production design for the Other World in *A Matter of Life and Death* (1946) by Hein Heckroth. (Hein Heckroth/© ITV/BFI National Archive)

Designs for the celestial trial in
A Matter of Life and Death (1946) by
Hein Heckroth. (Hein Heckroth/© ITV/
BFI National Archive)

A Matter of Life and Death culminates in a celestial trial observed by a vast audience of Allied servicemen and women from across the globe. It provides a powerful vision of international unity during fractured political times. Pressburger's heavenly fantasy of equality (voiced through Kathleen Byron's angel: 'we're all the same up here') was unfortunately not the earthly reality for many serviceman who faced segregation and discrimination from their own sides. (Hein Heckroth/© ITV/BFI National Archive)

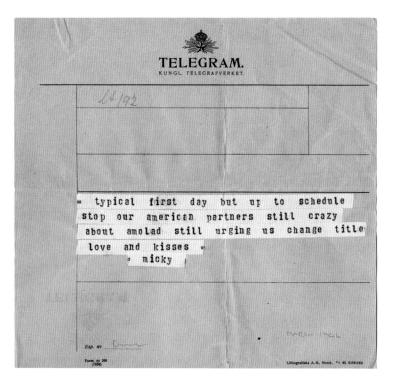

Telegram from Michael Powell to Emeric Pressburger during post-production of *A Matter of Life and Death* (1946). The film was eventually released in the US under the title *Stairway to Heaven*. (BFI National Archive)

Emeric Pressburger's handwritten script for *A Matter of Life and Death* (1946). (© Emeric Pressburger/ BFI National Archive)

Production design for Moy Castle in *I Know Where I'm Going!* (1945) by Alfred Junge.
(Alfred Junge/© ITV/The Harry Ransom Center)

Production design for the dream sequence in *I Know Where I'm Going!* (1945) by Alfred Junge.
(Alfred Junge/© ITV/La Cinémathèque française)

Location scouting sketch book for *Gone to Earth* (1950) by Ivor Beddoes. (Ivor Beddoes/©Disney/
BFI National Archive)

Production design for *Gone to Earth* (1950) by Hein Heckroth. (Hein Heckroth/© Disney/
Theaterwissenschaftliche Sammlung der Universität zu Köln)

Production design showing Hazel's pet fox for *Gone to Earth* (1950) by Ivor Beddoes.
(Ivor Beddoes/© Disney/BFI National Archive)

Poster for *Gone to Earth* (1950). (BFI National Archive)

Promotional material artwork for *Gone to Earth* (1950) by Ivor Beddoes. (Ivor Beddoes/©Disney/BFI National Archive)

Storyboard for *Gone to Earth* (1950) by Ivor Beddoes. (Ivor Beddoes/© Disney/BFI National Archive)

Notes from a Production Designer

Sarah Greenwood

Powell and Pressburger shape what we all do today as filmmakers. Their worlds are fascinating and always present, like a historic, beautiful background. It's hard to pinpoint specific references but when I look back I can see how so much of what they did can also be felt in what I've done, particularly in my films with the director Joe Wright. My work is realistic but it takes some of that magic and runs with it, highlights it, pulls it out.

When I worked with Joe, we didn't set out to make *Anna Karenina* (Joe Wright, 2012) as it was made, but I knew that there was something that Joe was after. It came down to the fact that we couldn't afford to shoot it conventionally because we couldn't afford to go to Russia. Turning on a sixpence, we decided that we were going to set it all in a derelict

Production design for *Anna Karenina* (Joe Wright, 2012) by Eva Kuntz and Sarah Greenwood (Eva Kuntz, Sarah Greenwood/© Working Title/Collection of the artist)

theatre. The only line that screenwriter Tom Stoppard changed in the script was 'this all takes place in a derelict theatre'. Everything else was exactly as it was, and we simply maintained the truth of it, whittling each scene down to the barest minimum and then layering it back up. We asked, where does it live; how does it work? Once we'd found the key to it, applying it through the film was a really interesting challenge, and one not unfamiliar to Powell and Pressburger. The painted cloth telling the story is very much in their ethos; not a slavish copy, but a truth to our film that finds a kindred spirit in theirs.

A filmmaker's work can have elements of theatre, but the language is that of cinema. It's all in camera. I like to play with scale and play with models. I love to travel within a film. For *Anna Karenina*, we built a beautiful train set for the son of Dolly Oblonskaya to play with. The characters step through a doorway and they're now on that train, moving through the countryside. Film allows you to play with scale in that way, taking viewers into the exquisite train carriage with Oblonskaya. You suspend disbelief; you truly believe that that beautiful carriage is inside that little train and going down that track which is going through the Russian countryside. It's about layers of belief that take you to a truth. Were it not for Powell and Pressburger I'm not sure you'd have the nerve to do that. You know that you can always go back to your filmmaking predecessors, and so much is there waiting for you. And the fact that it is there gives you permission to do these extraordinary things – because you know they did it first, and it worked. That's what they've given us.

When you're doing a new film you always key into something. That could be many things. It could be a character, a colour, a texture, a mood, a place. But you always focus in on a detail, and this can quite often be colour. At the time of writing, I'm filming *Cyrano* (Joe Wright, 2021) in Noto, Italy, where the entire city is a beautiful biscuit colour. Everything else has to work from or against or with the colour of biscuit; from habits to orbs. It's one of those unchangeable things that shapes the film. *Atonement* (Joe Wright, 2007) is about the green. Green is a really critical colour that has to be chosen, it can't just be allowed to seep in arbitrarily. *Atonement* begins in a summer that is overripe: ripe to the point of rottenness. We chose to saturate it in green; the green of the gardens, the green of the kitchen; everything from the architraves to the walls to the floor. And then there is Celia's (Kiera Knightley) green dress. That was Joe's idea and Jacqueline Durran's creation, and everything about it was right. It just pinged in the film, even though we'd used green everywhere else. That, for me, is how you use green. Red is the other colour, and one that Powell and Pressburger used very cleverly; those splashes of red. You use red and green very particularly and you use them for effect. Their presence is never arbitrary. There has to be a balancing within the shot.

Above and opposite: Haley Bennett as Roxanne, Peter Dinklage as Cyrano and Kelvin Harrison Jr. as Christian in *Cyrano* (Joe Wright, 2021), photographed by Peter Mountain. Mountain's photography animates the work being done by Greenwood's set to produce the distinct tones, textures and mood of the production. (Peter Mountain/© Metro-Goldwyn-Mayer Pictures Inc./BFI National Archive)

It's really interesting to think, had they had CGI at their fingertips, what else Powell and Pressburger might have done. They really knew their way around special effects, using them in a totally believable way. Particularly the visual effects [of W. Percy Day]. I always marvel at the fact that they hold on that opening shot in *Black Narcissus* (1947). The rule is you never hold on a special effect because you can see the brushmarks. But with Powell and Pressburger this bravery is precisely the point. It makes it so much more dramatic.

Filmmaking is ultimately founded on collaborative processes, and it doesn't stop in prep. A key collaborator for me as a designer is the director of photography. Together, you can bring so much to the production. The director/director of photography/designer is a critical triumvirate that defines the tenor of a production. When it works, as it does in their films, it is pure alchemy.

Sabu, photographed in character as Toomai for *Elephant Boy* (Robert J. Flaherty and Zoltan Korda, 1937) by Max Rosher. (Max Rosher/© ITV/BFI National Archive)

4

Black Narcissus

Mahesh Rao

As children, my sister and I would often be entertained by my father's stories of his own boyhood spent in Mysore in southern India. His family home was in a village eighty kilometres away and so he boarded with family friends in order to be able to go to a better school. The daily journey to school was made by horse-drawn tonga – and if the driver was in a pliant mood, he would allow one of the children to take the reins. Studies were often undertaken by the light of a hurricane lamp on a veranda. And only a few years prior, a boy called Sabu would have been working at the elephant stables that formed part of the huge Amba Vilas palace grounds in the heart of the city.

The contrast with our own modern lives was immense and my father enjoyed our wide-eyed absorption, perhaps an element of disbelief creeping into his own recollections of his past and how distant they seemed. 'Mysore Sabu', as my father called him, would crop up in these anecdotes from time to time. My father hadn't known anyone who had met Sabu but the story of a mahout's son who went on to become a Hollywood star was irresistible in those circles. The tale was told primarily for its outlandish quality – it was rare for Mysoreans to become stars in Bombay, let alone Los Angeles – but we could also sense an element of pride. Here was a real-life version of a rags-to-riches narrative that Sabu would go on to enact on screen in films like *The Thief of Bagdad* (1940), in which a scrappy thief goes on to become the Grand Vizier of Bagdad.

My sister and I never had an opportunity to see any of Sabu's films as children and we were of course too young to appreciate fully the nature of the roles that would have been available to an Indian actor like Sabu in Britain and Hollywood during the 1930s and

1940s. At the time we contented ourselves with the fact that a boy from Mysore had made it big. He had probably held court in a Beverly Hills mansion, the icons of the day guffawing at his jokes, the water in the kidney-shaped swimming pool winking in the sun.

Almost two decades later I saw Sabu in a film for the first time at a screening of *Black Narcissus* (1947) in London. I had little knowledge of the film's plot or the role he played in it. Adapted from the 1939 novel by Rumer Godden, the film tells the story of a group of nuns, led by the self-possessed Sister Clodagh and charged with a mission to set up a new convent, school and dispensary in a palace, nestled in a remote nook of the Himalayas. With the assistance of the local British agent, the suggestive and sardonic Mr Dean, they attempt to fulfil their objectives while struggling with their own inner turmoil, precipitated by the alien landscape that surrounds them. They are continually unsettled by the silent meditations of an ever-present holy man, the overtures of the Young General whose un-cle owns the palace, and the locals who seem never to appreciate the good fortune of the nuns' presence. As the troubled and disgruntled Sister Ruth becomes ever more infatuated with Mr Dean and suspicious of Sister Clodagh, the nuns' mission is derailed, the tensions and uncertainties building to a terrible climax. The film performed well at the box office, in spite of reviewers who were wary of its melodrama or convoluted story and reserved praise mainly for its technical qualities.[1] The choice of subject and setting was after all 'an astute move'[2], a recognition of the commercial gains to be made by portrayals of a vivid and exotic India, even as Britain was forced to give up its cherished colony that same year.

The film's melodrama and stunning backdrops notwithstanding, the first time that I saw the film, my eyes sought Sabu. He plays the Young General and makes his entrance thundering up to the palace at Mopu on a horse, eager to meet Sister Clodagh, the Sister Superior of the new convent. He shimmers with jewels and brocade from head to toe. The effect is not one of opulence but of an enthusiastic rummage in the dressing-up box. Indeed, even Rumer Godden saw the costumes of the Young General and his uncle, de-signed by Hein Heckroth, as inauthentic, or as she put it: 'pantomime clothes.'[3]

From the very outset Sabu's character declares to Sister Clodagh: 'you don't need to count me as a man.' The convent only teaches children and young women and the Young General is determined to convince the nun that he will fit into this scheme. He presents him-self as little more than an empty vessel to be filled with superior Western learning. His ea-

---

1.   Sarah Street, *Black Narcissus – British Film Guides* (London: Bloomsbury, 2005), 63.

2.   Macdonald, *Emeric Pressburger*, 265.

3.   Street, *Black Narcissus*, 18.

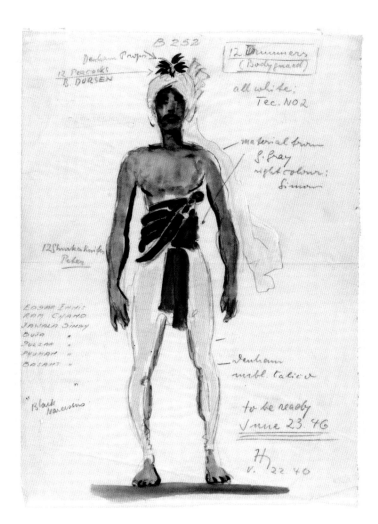

Costume design for *Black Narcissus* (1947) by Hein Heckroth. (Hein Heckroth/ ©ITV/BFI National Archive)

gerness to learn is played for comedy, with his unusual syntax and ingratiating zeal. There is an invitation to be charmed by this enthusiastic man-boy but it comes edged with ridicule.

It was quite a shock to see this representation of someone who seemed strangely familiar from family lore. As the film continued, I could sense myself shrinking in my seat whenever Sabu reappeared on screen. There seemed to be something fallacious about his conduct around the nuns and his apparent admiration even for the dissolute Mr Dean. His character repeatedly denied his own selfhood and the actor seemed damningly complicit in this portrayal. Our first encounter was a profound disappointment. Could this curiously sexless figure, cloying and obsequious, really be the hero of my father's tales of the famed star from Mysore?

Design for the scenic backdrops in *Black Narcissus* (1947) by Ivor Beddoes. (Ivor Beddoes/©ITV/BFI National Archive)

What made the experience even more dissonant was that *Black Narcissus* is a film that is suffused with sex, the memory of it, the fascination with it, the fear of it. Powell and Pressburger ensure that hardly anyone escapes the strange consequences of being transplanted into this land of enigma and incitement. Sister Ruth's vulnerability and subsequent breakdown are the most extreme representations of Mopu's sexualising effect but many others are made explicit. Cracks soon appear in Sister Clodagh's cool exterior as memories of her previous life intrude upon her: the pulsing thrill of being on a hunt with her lover, casting out her rod in a sun-dappled lake as though she could reel in her rosy future. Mr Dean is almost always clad in his indecently short shorts, sometimes shirt unbuttoned to the waist, a salty remark at hand to accompany his bold sneer. Even clearheaded and reliable Sister Philippa is diverted from her righteous course by the unsettling wildness of Mopu. 'I think you can see too far,' she says of the unfettered landscape that surrounds them. She too is revisited by

Production design for *Black Narcissus* (1947) by Ivor Beddoes. (Ivor Beddoes/© ITV/BFI National Archive)

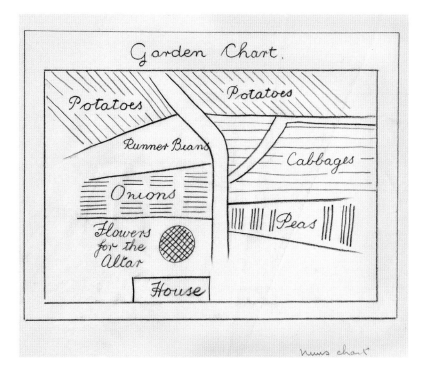

Design for Sister Philippa's garden planting chart, *Black Narcissus* (1947) by Ivor Beddoes. (Ivor Beddoes/© ITV/ BFI National Archive)

Production design by Ivor Beddoes for the wall murals at Mopu, *Black Narcissus* (1947), referencing its past life as a 'House of Women'. (Ivor Beddoes/©ITV/BFI National Archive)

long forgotten incidents, although we are not made privy to them. While not being permitted a specific sexual reawakening of her own, she plunges into the romance and rejuvenation of planting flowers instead of the potatoes and onions that the convent requires.

Going beyond these markers of plot and character, Powell and Pressburger take every care to ensure their cinematic universe establishes the inescapable eroticism of the East. We are told that the palace was once known as the House of Women and housed the concubines of the General's father. Our introduction to the interiors of the building begins with a faded mural of near naked men and women, rapt in admiration of each other's bodies. Dark alcoves and staircases suggest secret assignations. The presence of myriad lattices and balconies mean that any illicit acts also carry the danger of being spied upon. Long shadows suddenly slice across the screen. Above all, the unrelenting wind never ceases to carry its dark portents. Its whoosh is a constant presence through the film. And

The Palace of Mopu, *Black Narcissus* (1947) photographed by Max Rosher. (Max Rosher/© ITV/BFI National Archive)

even when we cannot hear it, we can see the tumult of dried leaves in the courtyard, the nuns' fluttering robes, vines that tremble, flickering lamplight, windows that slam shut.

The acting, script, Jack Cardiff's Technicolor cinematography and Alfred Junge's art direction (both of whom won Academy Awards for their work) all achieve an outstanding sublimation of this latent sexual energy. But in this seductive panorama, the Young General is denied any sexual presence or agency, including in the portrayal of his romance with Kanchi, an unruly village girl who has moved into the convent. He is infantilised whenever possible: even Angu Ayah, the servant at the palace, exhorts him in one scene to give Kanchi a beating as punishment for stealing and 'begin to become a man'. During the seduction scenes with Kanchi, there is a complete absence of chemistry: the Young General stands stiff and aloof, looking as though he is desperate to be elsewhere as she teasingly dashes around him. The prancing coquetry of a 'native girl' is of course to be expected from a film of this era. But having denied the Young General any kind of sexual identity,

The rocky outcrops of Mopu's Himalayan setting, recreated at Pinewood for *Black Narcissus* (1947). Photographed by Max Rosher. (Max Rosher/© ITV/BFI National Archive)

we are then asked to believe that he would be entranced by this girl and be prepared to run away with her, resolved to bear the resulting cost to his standing and status. Later, Sister Clodagh, while enumerating the strange intrusions that have disrupted all order in the convent – the holy man, the wind, the clear air, the mountains – also includes the presence of the Young General. It is hard to believe this of a man whose greatest passion seems to be his French conjugation. It is harder still to reconcile this portrayal with the character in Godden's book, in which the link between the Young General and Sister Clodagh's old lover is made wholly unambiguous: she dreams of them talking to each other, while she tries – and fails – to attract their attention.

The Young General's specific asexuality seems a curious choice for a film that takes its eroticism so seriously. But *Black Narcissus* is a film that imbues the East with sexual peril rather than freedom, a place where even a gentle relaxation of strictures can prove explosive. Nothing embodied this danger more than the body of the Black or brown man.

'Miscegenation' was expressly forbidden under the Motion Picture Production Code, which still existed at the time of the production of *Black Narcissus*. The makers of the film would have been acutely aware of the censors' gaze and, indeed, were compelled to make certain changes: American censors required the flashback to Sister Clodagh's love affair in Ireland to be cut,[4] under pressure from the Catholic Legion of Decency. What then would they have made of an Indian actor radiating sexual magnetism, surrounded as he would have been by white female actors, their tightly wound restraint slowly coming apart? And would Western audiences of the time have been prepared to see this on screen? Even twenty years later, Blake Edwards's *The Party* (1968) would feature an Indian male protagonist, naïve, blundering and sexless, another brown child-man, who posed no danger to the beautiful white women who surrounded him. In another sign of the times, the character was played by Peter Sellers in brownface.

If we move forward another seven years, we can see the emergence of another fictional representative of the Indian aristocracy but this time 'a Nawab in his prime,' said to be 'very manly and strong'. Ruth Prawer Jhabvala's 1975 Booker prize winning novel *Heat and Dust* also trades in an exotic India, its chapters peppered with descriptions of palaces, bazaars and beggars, acting as a gentle precursor to the wave of Raj nostalgia that swept over British film and television in the 1980s. But even though there is an abundance of local swindlers and enlightenment-seeking Westerners, Jhabvala is too skilled a writer not to land on some hard truths. As in *Black Narcissus*, a rich Indian of the ruling class comes into close contact with a group of white settlers in India, this time in the dry and dusty northern plains. But unlike the Young General, the handsome Nawab is a man of great sophistication and social ease who almost inevitably attracts the affections of Olivia, the bored and spoilt wife of the Assistant Collector: 'here at last was one person in India to be interested in her the way she was used to.'[5] In the Merchant Ivory film adaptation of the novel, naturally the Nawab is played by Shashi Kapoor, that most dashing and urbane of Indian stars of the time.

Not only does Olivia enter into a sexual relationship with the Nawab, she becomes pregnant by him, the Indian lover succeeding where the English husband failed. Even though she terminates her pregnancy, she is destined to pay the price for her transgressions by being abandoned by her social set and living a solitary life in the mountains. Years after Olivia's disgrace, one of her former neighbours publishes a monograph on his experiences in India. 'There are many ways of loving India, many things to love her

---

4. Powell, *A Life in Movies*, 585.

5. Ruth Prawer Jhabvala, *Heat and Dust* (London: Abacus 2011), 19.

for – the scenery, the history, the poetry, the music, and indeed the physical beauty of the men and the women – but all…are dangerous for the European who allows himself to love too much.'[6] The warning is clear: any admiration of and fascination for this bewitching country had to be tempered with caution. India would always be an adversary to be fought against, 'from without and, especially, from within: from within one's own being.' The character's words could almost be an explanation for the representation of the Young General that we see in *Black Narcissus*.

If the Young General's sexlessness feels like a jarring falsity at the heart of the film, another aspect of his characterisation feels disruptively true. He seizes every opportunity to play up to the nuns, desperate to seek their favour. In a key classroom scene, he draws out his handkerchief and takes great pains to explain to Sister Ruth that it is scented with a perfume called Black Narcissus, bought in the Army and Navy Stores in London. In a cliquish appeal he asks the woman who will only ever hold him in racist contempt: 'Don't you think it's rather common to smell of ourselves?' Almost all the other Indians are allowed their rebellions, however small: Kanchi's outrageous flirtation, Angu Ayah's flippant retorts, the villagers' refusal to return to the school or dispensary. But even after the Young General has taken Kanchi away, he returns to seek forgiveness from Sister Clodagh, hands clasped like a chastened schoolboy.

When you are part of a minority, it's almost inevitable that you bring a forensic scrutiny to the nature of representation that is taking place on screen, even when the film was made over 70 years ago. How will *they* see us? So, the sight of an Indian prince truckling to stony-faced and unreceptive British nuns is difficult to watch. But the discomfort doubles down. Many of us have known people, sometimes in our own families – perhaps we have even been those people – who have displayed this characteristic of the Young General. These are people who might not have flaunted their perfume to appeal to whiteness but there have always been many other things to display: accent, education, culture, aesthetics. These are people who may have denied some crucial part of their identity, the language they speak with their parents, the correct pronunciation of their name, the food laid out on their dinner tables, in order to avoid the commonness that comes with smelling of themselves. These are people we have known intimately. The cringe in the cinema seats reaches far into our lives.

The image of Sabu as the 'loyal native' was certainly not accidental, nor was it limited to his role in *Black Narcissus*. The great success of his early films, *Elephant Boy* (Robert Flaherty, Zoltan Korda, 1937) and *The Drum* (Zoltan Korda, 1938), turned him into an in-

---

6.   Ruth Prawer Jhabvala, *Heat and Dust*, 171.

stant star, their producer, Alexander Korda, ensuring that Sabu's face was used to sell not just posters and turbans but also boxes of Shredded Wheat. As one of the most renowned Indians in Britain at the time, Sabu's story could easily be packaged as a 'fetishized version of imperial containment and migrant assimilation' for a country confronting the beginning of the end of empire but wishing to be reassured about its continued influence and power over its colonies and subjects.[7] As a poor Indian stable boy who had been 'saved' and elevated to stardom, both in his film roles and in real life, Sabu could be portrayed as a dutiful and trustworthy young man, grateful to the pioneering white film makers and the British public that held him so close to their hearts. In fact, he was said to have gone further: at a London Films party in 1936, he toasted his British citizenship with the words, 'To hell with the bloody foreigners!'[8]

It is easy to imagine that it is only with years of hindsight that these tangled representations can be successfully unpicked. However, even as Sabu's career flourished, he would have been able to witness the effect of his choice of films on Indian audiences who were furious with the way they were portrayed. *The Drum* elicited negative reviews in the Indian press and led to riots in Bombay and Madras in 1938, particularly over the depiction of Pashtun communities in the North-West Frontier Province as cruel, debauched and treacherous. Seemingly undaunted, Sabu carried on, and by the time he was cast in *Black Narcissus*, his fee was £15,000, not much less than the £18,000 paid to Deborah Kerr to star in the leading role of Sister Clodagh.[9] Sabu readily accepted the part of the Young General, fully aware that the jungle and fantasy films which had been his staple were no longer being made. In Michael Powell's own words (said with admiration): 'He knew very well that he had come from nowhere and he had no intention of ending up nowhere.'[10]

The need to show gratitude and loyalty to an adopted country would not have been far from the thoughts of Emeric Pressburger either. As a Hungarian immigrant, working with his compatriot Korda at London Films, he brought the detached, careful observations of an outsider to his screenplays, but he would have been all too conscious of the precariousness of his position in the British film world. Once again, the danger of smell-

---

7. Jacqueline Gold, 'Civilizing Sabu of India' in *India in Britain: South Asian Networks and Connections 1858–1950*, (ed.) Susheila Nasta (London: Palgrave Macmillan 2012), 181.

8. Ibid., 186.

9. Macdonald, *Emeric Pressburger*, 267.

10. Powell, *A Life in Movies*, 580.

Kathleen Byron as Sister Ruth in
Black Narcissus (1947) by Max
Rosher. (Max Rosher/©ITV/
BFI National Archive)

ing too much of himself would have been clear. After his retirement he commented to cinematographer Chris Challis: 'I am much more English than you are. You were born English, but I chose to be.'[11]

Black Narcissus was made to discomfit its audiences. And by focusing on (white) female desire and repression in such a bold and unflinching way, it succeeds in its remit. The apogee of this scrutiny reaches us in Sister Ruth's final scenes, where different elements converge to create a sequence of almost unbearable tension. The shot of Sister Ruth's eyes, red-rimmed and verging on bestial, as she spies on Sister Clodagh; mysterious creaks and flitting shadows; Brian Easdale's roiling score which builds to a heart-stopping choral crescendo; the pink and orange light that lingers on the edges of the frames, suggesting the

---

11. Macdonald, *Emeric Pressburger*, 393.

emotional inferno to come: the compression of all these effects into a relentless few minutes results in a profoundly disturbing end to the expression of female yearning and passion.

But many years later, the film also manages to generate unease of a different order. Its exoticisation of India, partly by the other-worldly tones of its visual palette, and partly by its depiction of characters like the Young General and Kanchi, makes for uncomfortable viewing. Perhaps most disturbing of all is that I continue to be mesmerised by a film that confounds and troubles. In spite of its flaws, there are so many compelling reasons to return to the film. The psychodrama of a tiny community with rigid rules is instantly recognisable to anyone who has had to experience such a life. Unfolding like a fever dream, the inner lives of the film's protagonists are gradually revealed in a hallucinatory haze, as caution sounds in the background, whether from the steady beat of the local drums or the fervent ring of the convent's bell. The shocks, even when previously registered, continue to captivate: the shot of Sister Philippa's horribly overworked and calloused hands, the manic transformation of Sister Ruth's face as she accuses Sister Clodagh of lusting after Mr Dean.

Poster for *Black Narcissus* (1947) by Eric Pulford. (Eric Pulford/BFI National Archive)

There is a wonderful sense of possibility in the film's narrative: that a hand can at any time reach down and disturb the long-settled silt of a staid life. Closed worlds can be prised open. In spite of the specificity of time and place, there remains a universality to these themes. At the beginning of the film, Sister Clodagh says that to serve voluntarily is the greatest strength of their Order. But what are we to make of this strength by the end of the film? Powell and Pressburger apply a fierce rigour to the psychological trajectory of the nuns, and while the final retreat from Mopu may seem elegiac and steeped in failure, we are also left wondering what kind of transformation has been worked on Sister Clodagh and the others. Mr Dean observes towards the end of the film that Sister Clodagh has become more human – and we are transported to that earlier image of a young woman casting out her rod in a lake as though she wished to reel in her rosy future, a woman who had shown her small town in Ireland that she could love.

Also irresistible is the film's visual language. The sky is of the precise piercing blue required to convey the heady altitude and the thinness of the air. Rhododendrons and azaleas blaze into view enhancing the impression of an unexpected vision, a sudden entry into a place of such thrilling prospects that even the most mundane objects thrum with colour. Pale jagged peaks in the distance and dizzying views from precipices mimic the turmoil in the characters' inner lives. While we can take issue with the late-empire tropes that underpin this particular story, the film cannot be faulted on its brilliant distillation of the effect that place can have on the human psyche. Encoded within its rich purples and startling azures is the profound power of landscape as history, memory and metaphor.

It is worth noting that in spite of its intense engagement with a sense of place, the film nonetheless reduces the nuns' relationship with Mopu into a flat binary: to stay or to leave. Godden's book confronts the issue of the presence of settlers in India in a different way: *how* are they to stay. This is hardly surprising given Godden's interest in a continuing British presence there, having spent her childhood in India and having returned there after her schooling in the UK. Her early years passed in a vast mansion in Narayanganj (now in Bangladesh) when she was kept strictly apart from Indians who were not family servants. She later insisted on lessons on Hinduism and 'being allowed to visit Indians and to speak to them.'[12]

The legal, territorial and socio-cultural contours of British life in India emerge consistently throughout Godden's *Black Narcissus*. Early chapters stress that the land around Mopu

---

12. Peter Guttridge, 'Obituary: Rumer Godden', *The Independent*, 11 November 1998, Available online: https://www.independent. co.uk/arts-entertainment/obituary-rumer-godden-1184108.html (Date accessed: 19 Jan 2021)

does not form part of the General's State but has been leased from the British and, later, Sister Clodagh clings to the issue of rights of way, questioning the practice of local villagers who visit the holy man on what she considers 'our grounds'. Mr Dean, as an old India hand, is of course far more adept at negotiating the complex terrain of 'how they are to stay'. In one remarkable scene in the book, which failed to make it to the screen, he is presented with plans for a chapel at Mopu, a replica of the chapel at the Order's headquarters in Sussex: the same tiled dado, the same window above the altar of the Flight into Egypt.[13] Mr Dean casts an unimpressed eye over the drawings and returns the next day with his own plans for a chapel. It is one of the few occasions in the book when he drops his impertinent and distancing demeanour; instead, he is enthusiastic and sincere. His plans show a structure high above the valley, with 'not exactly walls and not exactly pillars', where the clouds and snows can be seen, stories in local writing to be painted on the outside, straw on the floor to encourage people to rest, and a bell secured under a dome. 'It's more like a temple,' exclaims Sister Briony and, of course, this is entirely the point. Mr Dean is no stranger to an astute and insidious assertion of power that recognises local customs and beliefs as well as the syncretism of India's religions. It is also an assertion that knows very well that nothing will actually be ceded: the land will still be occupied, the missionary zeal will continue, the urge to 'civilise' will be unabated. That, he suggests, is how they are to stay. The nuns reject the plans and he tears them up. When the nuns eventually leave, the book and the film converge again, the rains arriving as though to wash away every trace of their presence.

Little in *Black Narcissus* is really as it seems. The entire film was shot in England and so peaks delicately painted on glass stand in for the Himalayas, a sub-tropical garden in Horsham passes for Indian mountainous forests, and a set at Pinewood Studio comes to be the palace at Mopu. Tricks and contradictions abound in its construction. A film steeped in Orientalist notions and imperial fantasies also lays bare the instability of the colonial enterprise and the barrenness of ideas of superior Western learning and evangelism. Seen through one prism, the characters can seem false and artificial; through another, complex harbingers of uncomfortable truths. Frequently the film obscures any sense of realism and yet also manages to dispel one or two long cherished myths. Any certainty about the film shifts like the hues on the walls of the palace at Mopu. Perhaps the only true certainty is that I will watch the film again.

---

13.   Rumer Godden, *Black Narcissus* (London: Virago, 2013), 152.

Design for the scenic backdrops in *Black Narcissus* (1947) by Ivor Beddoes. *Black Narcissus*' vertiginous Himalayan setting and deliberately artificial vision of India was woven together in Alfred Junge's Pinewood studios sets, in Leonardslee sub-tropical gardens in Sussex, in scale models of the convent and through matte paintings by veteran effects wizard W. Percy Day. As Powell said, 'The atmosphere in this film is everything and we must create and control it from the start. Wind, the altitude, the beauty of the setting – it must all be under our control.'
(Ivor Beddoes/© ITV/BFI National Archive)

The construction of the bell tower (left) in *Black Narcissus*; the realised bell tower (right). Photographed by Max Rosher.
(Max Rosher/©ITV/BFI National Archive)

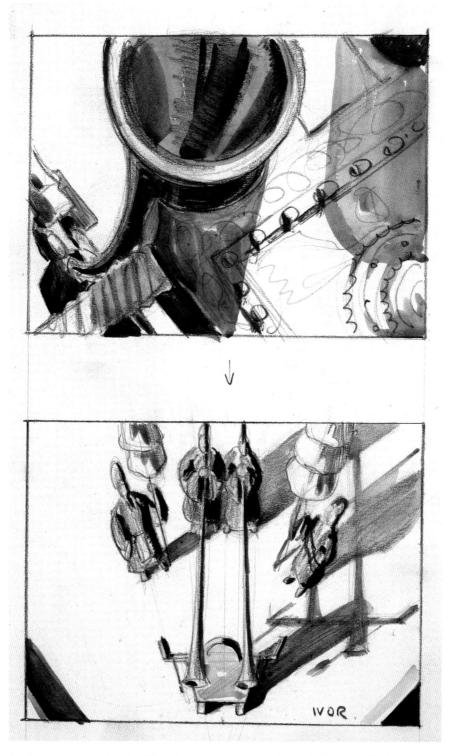

Continuity drawings, showing different camera perspectives for the bell tower in *Black Narcissus* (1947) by Ivor Beddoes. (Ivor Beddoes/© ITV/BFI National Archive)

sleeves of gown can be fastened over hand

gown to be worn over habit

fastened in back

sleeve of habit

belt starts here and closed in front

pocket in front

white linen or cotton

or the gown in blue or grey material in short

25. II.

1946

Above: Costume design for a nun's habit, *Black Narcissus* (1947) by Hein Heckroth. (Hein Heckroth/© ITV/BFI National Archive)

Opposite: Mopu's dinner table in *Black Narcissus* (1947), photographed by Max Rosher (top). Production design for the same scene (bottom), by Alfred Junge. The perilous, dislocated atmosphere in *Black Narcissus* is heightened by the film's continued visual refrain of having characters observe others from above, used from early on as Mother Dorothea and Sister Clodagh look down on the other sisters. The vantage, and Sister Ruth's ominously empty place, suggest her psychological separation from others and hint at trouble ahead. (Max Rosher/© ITV/BFI National Archive; Alfred Junge/© ITV/La Cinémathèque française)

Deborah Kerr as Sister Clodagh (top) in *Black Narcissus* (1947). (©ITV/BFI National Archive); The sisters of *Black Narcissus* (1947), photographed by George Cannons (above). Many stills of the 1940s and 50s were shot in black and white, to feed a predominantly monochrome print culture – even if the production was in colour. However, for a number of films, Powell and Pressburger pursued colour photography. Cannon's Kodachrome images differ in tone from the Technicolor process, but present an equally vibrant vision of India. (George Cannons/©ITV/BFI National Archive)

Above: Costume design for *Black Narcissus* (1947) by Hein Heckroth. (Hein Heckroth/© ITV/ Theaterwissenschaftliche Sammlung der Universität zu Köln)

Left: Poster for the Polish release of *Black Narcissus* (1947, poster produced 1957) by Henryk Tomaszewski. (© Henryk Tomaszewski/ BFI National Archive)

Storyboard drawings for *Black Narcissus* (1947) by Ivor Beddoes. (Ivor Beddoes/©ITV/BFI National Archive)

Above left: Budget sheet for *Black Narcissus* (1947), showing prinicipal actors' fees. (BFI National Archive)

Above right: Art department staff listing for *Black Narcissus* (1947). A myriad of hidden hands and minds worked under Alfred Junge. This staff listing – for just one section of the art department – hints at the scale of hidden labour that went into each production. (BFI National Archive)

Right: Deborah Kerr as Sister Clodagh in *Black Narcissus* (1947), photographed by Max Rosher. (© Estate of Max Rosher/BFI National Archive)

Above: The chapel at Mopu,
Black Narcissus (1947),
photographed by Max Rosher.
(Max Rosher/© ITV/BFI
National Archive)

Left: Creating the weather
of *Black Narcissus* (1947),
photographed by Max Rosher.
(Max Rosher/© ITV/BFI
National Archive)

Storyboard drawings for *Black Narcissus* (1947) by Ivor Beddoes. (Ivor Beddoes/© ITV/BFI National Archive)

Storyboard drawings for *Black Narcissus* (1947) by Ivor Beddoes. (Ivor Beddoes/©ITV/BFI National Archive)

Scenic artist Vishwanath Nageshkar (above), photographed by Max Rosher, realising the wall paintings for the Palace of Mopu, *Black Narcissus* (1947), based on production designs (below) by Ivor Beddoes. (Max Rosher/©ITV/ BFI National Archive; Ivor Beddoes/©ITV/BFI National Archive)

Production designs for *Black Narcissus* (1947) by Ivor Beddoes, showing (below) the holy man..
(Ivor Beddoes/©ITV/BFI National Archive)

Notes from an Artist

Michelle Williams Gamaker

My practice as an artist embodies 'fictional activism'; a term developed to interrogate agency within filmmaking, and to reflect on who gets to star in and make films. My *Dissolution* trilogy (2017–9) responds to some of the more intriguing questions within *Black Narcissus* (1947), asking what it might mean to restore performers of colour from marginalised characters in the first half of the twentieth century, to central figures in the here and now.

In 1946, auditions were held for the character of the silent dancing girl Kanchi in *Black Narcissus*. In a nationwide search, close to 1,000 hopefuls applied, with over 200 girls screen tested and interviewed. The coveted role finally went to seventeen-year-old Jean Simmons, who had recently won worldwide acclaim for her performance as the young Estella in David Lean's *Great Expectations* (1946). To fulfil the role, the white English actor had to wear dark panstick make-up and a jewel in her nose to become the 'exotic temptress' of Rumer Godden's novel of the same name.

Opposite: Jean Simmons, photographed in character as Kanchi, on the set of *Black Narcissus* (1947) by George Cannons. The typical work of a stills photographer is to depict moments and performances through still imagery, as if they have been taken directly from the film. But 'stills' actually result from the careful restaging of a key scene in front of a professional photographer. Occasionally, either through a special commission or through artistic practice, there is a noticeable deviation from the film text. Here, Cannons has created a standalone portrait using the set as a backdrop, with heavy blue filters added to the lighting. This gives the scene an icy glow, consequently altering Kanchi's/Simmons' appearance. The resultant photograph feels both a part of, and apart from, the film. (George Cannons/© ITV/BFI National Archive)

House of Women (2017) recasts the role, auditioning only Indian ex-pat or first-generation British Asian women and non-binary individuals living in the UK. Unlike the original role, for *House of Women* the re-cast Kanchi of the 21st Century *speaks*. Shot on 16mm film, the four candidates, Jasdeep Kaur Kandola, Arunima Rajkumar, Taranjit Mander and Krishna Istha, introduce themselves to an anonymous reader (voiced by Kelly Hunter) and recite a personalised alphabet including references to the history of photography and gender politics.

The Fruit is There to Be Eaten (2018) echoes the style of *Black Narcissus* in that it is set in India, but replaces painted backdrops with back projection and revealed sets to reimagine the relationship between lower-caste dancing girl Kanchi and missionary nun Sister Clodagh. In a schoolroom and the gardens of a Himalayan convent, Kanchi and Clodagh recognise they are trapped in a film set in 2017. With the colonies a distant memory, Clodagh's role as Sister Superior is redundant. This allows Kanchi to refuse the tutelage offered by their Mission, restating her Queered alphabet from *House of Women*. Kanchi also introduces her gods to Clodagh in order to challenge an imposed belief system, and in so doing to break down the so-called civility and benevolence of the Sisters into a space of desire and equality.

The Eternal Return (2019) moves beyond Powell and Pressburger's films to posit a now-struggling international film star Sabu in 1952 (who co-stars alongside Simmons in

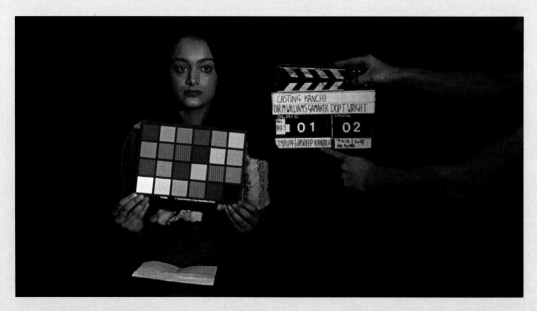

Jasdeep Kandola in *House of Women* (2017) by Michelle Williams Gamaker. (©Michelle Williams Gamaker/ Collection of the artist)

Black Narcissus) as he supports his family by performing in Tom Arnold's Christmas Circus in Haringey Arena. With the inclusion of 1950s British Pathé footage of circuses in Britain and their parading of tame beasts as 'exotic entertainment', the film shows the indignity Sabu felt by being similarly deployed in this context. The film also explores the notion of success in the absence of agency as it imagines the resentment of an individual for whom the price of fame was to be typecast. In Sabu's case, this was the frequent conflation of his background and career with a seemingly inescapable relationship with elephants; the animals recur throughout his filmography (the result of his debut performance in *Elephant Boy* 1937). In spite of his extraordinary fame, Sabu, I suggest, ultimately had little control over the roles he played during the course of his career.

The Fruit is There to be Eaten (2017) by Michelle Williams Gamaker. (© Michelle Williams Gamaker/ Collection of the artist)

Costume design for Conductor 71 (Marius Goring) in *A Matter of Life and Death* (1946) by Hein Heckroth. (Hein Heckroth/© ITV/BFI National Archive)

5

Starved for Technicolor

Sarah Street

'One is starved for Technicolor up there', sighs Conductor 71 (Marius Goring), the heavenly collector of the dead in *A Matter of Life and Death* (1946). Struck by the arresting beauty of a luscious and deeply saturated magenta rhododendron bush he encounters on earth, Conductor 71's wistful response is explained by the fact that he normally resides in a monochrome world of the afterlife, whereas the film's earthly sequences are shot in vivid colour. Released just after the end of the Second World War, the film's dual chromatic premise can also be related to the relative scarcity of Technicolor films at that time. In 1946, of the 532 films released in British cinemas only 42 were in colour, and only six of these were produced by British companies.[1] Technicolor was expensive, and the supply of its unique, three-strip cameras was limited. The idea that colour is all the more impressive when contrasted with its absence applies to more than the film's design. It confirms a commitment to colour as an active, conscious stylistic choice, as Powell stated in his autobiography: 'If you are a film-maker, you think in black and white or you think in colour. The Archers thought in colour from *The Thief of Bagdad* onwards'.[2]

Powell and Pressburger's films were central to the development of Technicolor in Britain and with the exception of *The Small Back Room* (1949) and *Ill Met by Moonlight* (1956), all of their post-war films are in colour. These were associated with a 'British School' of Technicolor, an approach admired by critics in Britain, France and the USA that was noted for its restrained, or painterly qualities. A delicate balance was struck by exploring chromatic variation, emphasis and spectacle within a restrained palette, as distinct from Hollywood's

---

1. Sarah Street, *Colour Films in Britain: The Negotiation of Innovation, 1900–55* (London: British Film, 2012), 258.
2. Michael Powell, *Million-Dollar Movie* (London: Heinemann, 1992), 35.

Production design for the bathhouse in *The Life and Death of Colonel Blimp* (1943) by Alfred Junge. (Alfred Junge/
© ITV/BFI National Archive)

often more assertive, even garish use of colour, particularly in musicals. Together with cinematographers, art directors, costume designers and other collaborators, Powell and Pressburger demonstrated how colour can be used expressively in film, particularly through the
idea of the 'composed film' in which music, colour and action combine to produce 'total'
effects. Beyond being colour-conscious, each film was subject to a specific approach which
displayed different facets of chromatic innovation on screen.

The Archers' first colour production was *The Life and Death of Colonel Blimp* (1943). Powell described it as 'a black and white film coloured'. It was guided by the idea of an overall
colour restraint with punctuating embellishment (for example, red lapels and insignia on
khaki uniforms). Its tripartite structure of three historical periods – 1902, 1918 and 1942 –
called for carefully differentiated colour accents. The first section, set mainly in Germany,
used rich colours such as reds for military uniforms and as a punctuating colour for the Ho-
henzollern Café sequence. The First World War setting for the second section is, by contrast,

dominated by khaki uniforms, and an almost bleached-out appearance while the final section applies a more varied range of punctuating colours. To achieve this Powell and Pressburger employed technicians whose work in Technicolor was already distinguished. Cinematographer Georges Périnal had worked on *The Thief of Bagdad* (Ludwig Berger, Michael Powell, Tim Whelan, 1940) and cinematographer Jack Cardiff, who had shot a number of Technicolor documentary shorts and a feature film, was employed on the film's second unit.

The production designer was Alfred Junge, who had worked with Powell on four previous films. Junge avoided strong, florid shades and designed every set on a lower key than he expected the film to reproduce. Yet the colours nevertheless had to be interesting: 'I had to tempt the camera to make more of my colour scheme than the actual scheme itself did'.[3] In the bathing house sequence near the start of the film, for example, Junge's design communicates its steamy atmosphere and contrast between the flesh tones and the soldiers' dark uniforms as they intrude into the space (see opposite). His muted, almost monochromatic concepts for a deserted battlefield on Armistice Day bear a striking resemblance to war artist Paul Nash's paintings. In the film, Périnal's lighting created shafts of sunlight to illuminate the scene in a symbolic way, drawing the eye away from the detritus of conflict in the foreground. This middle section of the film contrasts with the more obtrusive colour palette of 1902, while the 1942 section includes a scene in which colour is used for dramatic ends. When ATS driver Angela 'Johnny' Cannon (Deborah Kerr) is driving Theo (Anton Walbrook) the car stops abruptly as the traffic lights change to red. As Angela recalls Colonel Candy, their mutual acquaintance, the red light reflected on her face appears to underscore her enthusiasm (see overleaf).

Powell's use of colour to delineate between the three characters played by Deborah Kerr was also achieved through her costumes designed by British film and theatrical costumier Matilda Etches. These reflected the changing circumstances for women, from 'the heavy material of the dresses and shirts, the enormous hats and all the paraphernalia to make a woman feel decorative and useless' of 1902, to the corset-free First World War, and the uniforms and Utility clothing of the Second World War.[4] Edith is first seen, for example, in a heavy, dark green coat with a large ermine collar and lapels. Her large hat is of the same green, embellished on top with a decorative bird which appears to almost lean into her forehead (see p. 103). Towards the end of this section her dress becomes more informal, youthful and vibrantly coloured, featuring details such as a wide, shiny red belt worn with a pink

---

3. Junge, A. 'The Art Director and his work', *The Artist*, April and May 1944.

4. Michael Powell, *A Life in Movies* (London: Heinemann, 1986), 406–07.

Angela 'Johnny' Cannon (Deborah Kerr), caught in the red glow of the traffic lights. From the 2012 restoration of *The Life and Death of Colonel Blimp* (1943). (Restored by the Academy Film Archive in association with the BFI, ITV Studios Global Entertainment Ltd., and The Film Foundation. Restoration funding provided by The Material World Charitable Foundation, the Louis B. Mayer Foundation, Cinema per Roma Foundation, and The Film Foundation. Restoration consultants: Martin Scorsese and Thelma Schoonmaker Powell). (© ITV/BFI National Archive)

and white striped blouse. Quite a visual shock is created when the 1918 section opens with its dark, almost bleached-out appearance. Costume, however, permits performative glimpses of red such as for lapels and decorations on uniforms and, strikingly, the red cross on the uniform worn by a nurse (Deborah Kerr) whose uncanny physical resemblance to Edith startles Candy. Johnny's practical, uniformed appearance in the final section completes the transformative cycle, the features of which have been clearly demarked through colour.

Jack Cardiff's 2nd Unit work on *Blimp* led to Powell asking him to shoot *A Matter of Life and Death*, a film which took colour contrast even further: 'We were going to play with Technicolor on the screen in a way that nobody had ever played before', recalled Powell.[5]

---

5. Ibid, 536.

Edith (Deborah Kerr), framed by her collar and hat. From the 2012 restoration of *The Life and Death of Colonel Blimp* (1943). (© ITV/BFI National Archive)

The structural division of monochrome for heaven and colour for earth drew attention to the impact of Technicolor. Films had done this before, delineating fantasy worlds in colour, most notably the sepia tones used for Kansas in *The Wizard of Oz* (Victor Fleming, 1939) contrasted with the spellbinding colours of Oz. *A Matter of Life and Death* reversed this idea, equating heaven with cerebral rationality as a place for debate, whereas earth was subject to emotion, sexuality and conflict underscored by vivid colour schemes. Care was, however, taken to reduce the shock of the shifts between black and white and colour by filming the transition shots in Technicolor but then printing out the colour: an idea suggested by the laboratories. This achieved what Cardiff termed 'Technicolor black and white' which 'had this sort of strange look about it – not pure black and white, but with rather an iridescent sheen on it like a beetle's wing'.[6]

---

6. Justin Bowyer, *Conversations with Jack Cardiff: Art, Light and Direction in Cinema* (London: Batsford, 2003), 60.

Production design for the Stairway to Heaven in *A Matter of Life and Death* (1946) by Alfred Junge. (Alfred Junge/© ITV/BFI National Archive)

Cardiff collaborated on *A Matter of Life and Death* with operator Geoff Unsworth and focus puller Chris Challis. Alfred Junge was production designer, and Hein Heckroth designed the costumes. Cardiff recalled how Powell welcomed collaboration: 'He nearly always accepted any ideas I put forward with enthusiastic support'.[7] One such idea was his use of a lemon rather than an amber filter on the arc lights for a table-tennis scene when the frame freezes to indicate that the unreal, 'other' world, with its different time and look, has arrived.[8] The film was shot at Denham Studios but also featured exterior locations at Saunton Sands in North Devon. It was important to establish a credible setting which could at first be mistaken for heaven by Peter (David Niven) when he is washed up by the tide, having bailed out of his plane without a parachute. This strategy, of making some of

---

7. Jack Cardiff, *Magic Hour* (London: Faber and Faber, 1996), 85.

8. Bowyer, *Conversations with Jack Cardiff*, 62.

Production design for the operating theatre in *A Matter of Life and Death* (1946) by Alfred Junge.
(Alfred Junge/© ITV/BFI National Archive)

the earthly sets strange, added to the film's colour-driven slippage between its two worlds, reinforcing the notion that the boundaries between them are not distinct.

Junge's designs for the Stairway to Heaven included drawings in full colour, although these concepts did not feature in the final film. The stairway was instead shot in heavenly tones of black and white. But the transition scene between the two worlds, when Peter is being wheeled into the operating theatre, included a vivid colour effect that transports him to the other world. The close-up of his eye closing as the anaesthetic takes hold is one of a succession of images which de-familiarise the 'real' world. This is followed by a shot of pure colour: reds, pinks and purples combine with the sensation of movement within the frame. The camera is static but what passes before it is a wash of colour rolling upwards, eventually becoming monochrome as it transforms into Junge's drawing of figures gathering for the celestial court, completing the shot. This is then animated into the figures in heaven as the fully black and white world assumes dominance. This is a spectacular example of colour being used to carry both character and audience into another world.

Production designs for the bell tower at Mopu in *Black Narcissus* (1947) by Alfred Junge. (Alfred Junge/© ITV/ La Cinémathèque française)

The Archers' following films – *Black Narcissus* (1947), *The Red Shoes* (1948), *Gone to Earth* (1950), *The Elusive Pimpernel* (1950) and *The Tales of Hoffmann* (1951) realised Powell's aim to 'go even further, and further again' with colour, particularly using it as expressive of emotion and atmosphere.[9] *Black Narcissus* is widely regarded as one of the finest Technicolor films, inspiring a number of filmmakers including Martin Scorsese, Michael Giaimo and Bong Joon-ho.[10] The studio-controlled environment, combined with location

9.   Powell, *A Life in Movies*, 536.

10. Smith, G. (1998), 'Street smart: Excerpts from Martin Scorsese interviews', *Film Comment*, vol. 34, no. 3: 68–77; Desowitz, B. (2013), 'Immersed in Movies: First Look: Designing the Winter Wonderland of *Frozen*', *Indiewire*, 7 Oct 2013. https://indiewire. com/2013/10/immersed-in-movies-first-look-the-winter-wonderland-of-frozen-122606/ (accessed 15 June 2020); Joon-ho, B. (2020), 'Memories of… British Cinema', *Sight and Sound*, vol. 30, no. 3: 33.

shooting at Leonardslee Gardens, West Sussex, permitted the film's technical and creative teams to deliver the desired exotic atmosphere for its simulated Himalayan location. Junge was once again production designer, and his designs envisaged the spectacular location of the palace at Mopu, where the nuns establish a school and dispensary. His sketches locate Mopu high among the mountains, with a vertiginous drop that becomes a central location in the film's dramatic conclusion when Sister Ruth (Kathleen Byron) falls to her death. Matte artist and special effects technician W. Percy Day created the sheer drop, incorporating a new, economical method for the matte process which dispensed with shooting tests before the actual shooting of scenes.[11] Painted glass shots were also used to create the impression of the seductive, exotic exterior landscape that disturbs the nuns, threatening to deviate them from their mission. Comparing the sketches, set and final scene shows the supreme artistry that was achieved.

The declared influence of painters such as Caravaggio and Vermeer can be seen in Jack Cardiff's cinematography, particularly the effective use of chiaroscuro lighting. The Vermeer effect was anticipated by Junge, as shown in the design for the schoolroom (see overleaf and p. 119). The natural effect of light streaming through a window is used, as in Vermeer's paintings, to illuminate the figure, also shadows sculpting detail in subtle ways. Cardiff applied fog filters and diffusing techniques for the 'stalking' scene towards the end of *Black Narcissus*, when Clodagh goes to ring the bell at dawn, just before she is apprehended by Ruth from whose viewpoint the scene is mostly conveyed. Brian Easdale's music adds a pulsating soundtrack to a sequence with no dialogue but which communicates through sound, colour and diffused light the impending tragic mood. Cardiff's fog filters and use of green filters in the filler light and also pinkish colours create expressive tones of pink, mauve and grey, as Ruth watches Clodagh from afar. Easdale composed the music before the sequence was shot. Powell recalled he 'insisted on rehearsing and shooting to a piano track and consulting Brian with a musical score in my hand over each set-up'.[12] This is an early instance of the Archers' use of the 'composed film', in which a film or sequence unites in a precise combination of editing, musical punctuation, movement within the frame, juxtaposition through lighting and colour. Powell likened it to opera 'in the sense that music, emotion, image and voices all blended together into a new and splendid whole'.[13]

---

11. Street, *Colour Films in Britain*, 180.

12. Powell, *A Life in Movies*, 583.

13. Ibid.

Storyboard drawing for *Black Narcissus* (1947) by Ivor Beddoes. (Ivor Beddoes/© ITV/BFI National Archive)

Cardiff was faced with challenges that required him to experiment with lighting for Technicolor. For the scenes that took place in candlelight, for example, he needed a considerable amount of light for the flames to be visible. His solution was to hang a lamp up above the candle. The light source could be manipulated from the spot rail above to create flickering effects but without the source being visible. Orange filters on the light with a dimmer also enabled Cardiff to take the brightness up and down.[14] Technicolor at first objected to the amount of diffusion on *Black Narcissus*, but the 'painterly' look of the film, its subtleties of mood and tone eventually won them over to its artistry. The arc lamps used on the film were big and unwieldy and diffusion had to be achieved with tracing paper and dimmer shutters. Even so, Cardiff acknowledged that the hard arc lighting nevertheless

---

14. Bowyer, *Conversations with Jack Cardiff*, 75.

Black Narcissus (1947). (© ITV)

'helped to suggest the crystal-clear mountain light, and the dramatic atmosphere needed for this fabulous Himalayan world'.[15]

Ivor Beddoes, a painter and designer who worked in the art department, made many wonderful painted sketches for *Black Narcissus* and subsequent Archers' films. His striking coloured sketch for the schoolroom scene anticipates how it was shot. For the costumes, Hein Heckroth contrasted the brightly coloured, embellished, silken fabrics and jewels worn by the Young General (Sabu) with the nuns' off-white habits (see p. 118). The film's reputation for experimenting with colour extended to the photography of George Frederic Cannons who shot stunning production stills in Kodachrome on the set of *Black Narcissus* at Pinewood. Cannons worked for Rank and at that time Kodachrome was not widely used by the Organisation.

---

15. Cardiff, *Magic Hour*, 88.

The Young General (Sabu) in *Black Narcissus* (1947). (© ITV)

The Red Shoes further explored the idea of the 'composed film'. As discussed in Chapter 6, the film united creative energies to produce another seminal film in which colour expression and symbolism were central. Jack Cardiff's cinematography was once again distinguished by technical experimentation, particularly for the ballet sequences when he accelerated the camera's speed to film dancers as they leapt in the air.[16] The production design was this time assigned to Hein Heckroth as the Archers' primary production designer after *Black Narcissus*, as Powell increasingly favoured Heckroth's anti-realist, painterly approach.[17] His 'colour score' for the ballet sequence in *The Red Shoes* ensured that colour effects and values were central to the ideals of the 'composed film' and can be seen as a study in the use of red for different, at times contradictory, meanings.[18]

16. Street, *Colour Films in Britain,* 188.

17. Moor, A. (2005), 'Hein Heckroth at the Archers: Art, Commerce, Sickliness', *Journal of British Cinema and Television,* vol. 2, no. 1: 70.

18. Street, *Colour Films in Britain,* 188–90.

Production design for
a background in
Gone to Earth (1950),
indicating colour palette,
by Ivor Beddoes.
(Ivor Beddoes/© Disney/
BFI National Archive)

The next three films, *Gone to Earth* (1950), *The Elusive Pimpernel* (1950) and *The Tales of Hoffmann* (1951), involved another change in collaborators. Chris Challis was promoted to cinematographer, with Heckroth now ensconced as production designer. While *Gone to Earth* does not involve the overt experimentation of previous or subsequent films, it uses colour expressively in its depiction of the rugged Shropshire landscape, and symbolically in its costuming, particularly for the film's heroine, Hazel (Jennifer Jones) (see overleaf). As a historical melodrama it makes use of low light levels for firelight interiors, and also under-exposed landscape shots with silhouetted figures against the sky that resemble *Gone with the Wind* (Victor Fleming, 1939), the classic Technicolor film produced by David O. Selznick who was executive producer on *Gone to Earth*. *The Elusive Pimpernel* used colour effectively in a historical drama. Heckroth used painted backdrops and *trompe l'oeil* effects rather than solid sets to foreground action and emphasise costumes.[19] This was part of a deliberate strategy to heighten their visual sumptuousness and colours. Powell was very satisfied with these effects, recalling: 'I did not think there had been such taste and control in a Technicolor picture',[20] likening *The Elusive Pimpernel* to *Becky Sharp* (Rouben Mamoulian, 1935), the first three-strip

19. Moor, A. (2005), 'Hein Heckroth at the Archers: Art, Commerce, Sickliness', *Journal of British Cinema and Television*, vol. 2, no. 1: 67–81.
20. Michael Powell, *Million-Dollar Movie*, 49.

Hazel's yellow dress in *Gone to Earth* (1950). (©Disney/BFI National Archive)

Technicolor feature film in which 'the settings are generally held to a range of cool neutrals and browns, allowing the characters to introduce more assertive colours'.[21] But it was *The Tales of Hoffmann*, an adaptation of Offenbach's opera, that pushed the Archers' fascination with colour even further to what Heckroth described as 'an exercise in pure colour'.[22]

Heckroth argued that colour should be used dramatically in film, and in *The Tales of Hoffmann* he worked with a set of colour ideas to underscore, as in music, the film's three tales, or sections. The first tale, concerning Hoffmann's love for Olympia (Moira Shearer) features yellow floating gauze, browns and glittering cellophane to convey a light-hearted, frivolous mood. The second act, set in Giulietta's Venetian palace, features purples, reds, blacks and golds to convey a rich, deeply saturated look. This contrasts with the sombre greys and blues of the last tale which deals with Hoffmann's love for consumptive singer Antonia (Ann Ayres), colour accents which again were carefully planned at the design stage. Chris Challis recalled how the theatrical sets were filmed using hand-made colour filters, gauzes and back lighting to achieve the variety of subtle colour effects. Within the film's tripartite design there was considerable play with colour, for example, the use of colour effects towards the end of the first part. Olympia's tale, coded primarily in yellows for

21. Scott Higgins, *Harnessing the Technicolor Rainbow: Color Design in the 1930s* (Austin: Texas University Press, 2007), 51.
22. Quoted in Keene, V. (1951), 'The man who designed', *Picturegoer*, 21 April: 16–17.

Production design for Act 3, *The Tales of Hoffmann* (1951) by Ivor Beddoes. (Ivor Beddoes/© STUDIOCANAL/ BFI National Archive)

most of its duration, uses the shock effect of a totally green screen to dramatise how Coppélius has been tricked by Spalanzani. The green screen indicates horror and Coppélius' determination to seek revenge; its impact is all the more shocking because it is followed by a shot that is almost drained of colour. A similar effect of using pure colour suffusion to signify trauma had been used previously in *Black Narcissus* when a red screen indicates Sister Ruth losing consciousness. The second act has a sumptuous palette which is enriched by the fabrics of the costumes, jewels and gauze curtains. Powell and Heckroth wanted to make colour 'talk' so that 'every mood and emotion has its shade'.[23] This can be seen especially by comparing the designs for the theatrical epilogue with how these were eventually filmed as a fantastical and visually sumptuous emblematic sequence of dancing figures.

---

23. Powell, M. and Heckroth, H. (1950), 'Making Colour Talk', *Kinematograph Weekly*, British Studio Supplement, 9 Nov, 5.

The Tales of Hoffmann (1951). (© STUDIOCANAL)

The demarcation of colours to illustrate spaces and moods was further experimented with in *Oh... Rosalinda!!* (1955), a CinemaScope musical-comedy that was again designed by Heckroth and shot by Challis. Since *The Battle of the River Plate* (1956), a VistaVision film shot by Challis, did not require an overly theatrical or stylised approach, Arthur Lawson took on the mantle of production designer, and Heckroth maintained a shaping influence in the role of artistic adviser. The film enjoyed commercial success, but as Powell and Pressburger's last colour collaboration it was a relatively restrained end to a cycle of films which truly advanced the structural, expressive and symbolic use of colour, and went on to inspire a generation of filmmakers. Resonances can be felt across films such as *The Duellists* (Ridley Scott, 1977), *Wings of Desire* (Wim Wenders, 1987), *The Age of Innocence* (Martin Scorsese, 1993), *Pleasantville* (Gary Ross, 1998) and the films of Derek Jarman. The Archers and their collaborators did indeed demonstrate what it meant to really think, talk and create colour for the screen.

Production design for the colour transition/Conductor 71's rose in *A Matter of Life and Death* (1946) by Alfred Junge. (Alfred Junge/©ITV/The Harry Ransom Center)

The Archers, photographed by Fred Daniels on the set of *The Life and Death of Colonel Blimp* (1943). Note the signed production design of the bathhouse by Alfred Junge (see p.100). (Fred Daniels/BFI National Archive)

The 2012 restoration of *The Life and Death of Colonel Blimp* (1943). (Restored by the Academy Film Archive in association with the BFI, ITV Studios Global Entertainment Ltd., and The Film Foundation. Restoration funding provided by The Material World Charitable Foundation, the Louis B. Mayer Foundation, Cinema per Roma Foundation, and The Film Foundation. Restoration consultants: Martin Scorsese & Thelma Schoonmaker Powell) (©ITV/BFI National Archive)

Production designs for the bell tower at Mopu in *Black Narcissus* (1947) by Alfred Junge. (Alfred Junge/©ITV/La Cinémathèque française)

Mopu's Himalayan setting, recreated at Pinewood for *Black Narcissus* (1947). (© ITV)

Production designs for the bell tower at Mopu in *Black Narcissus* (1947) by Alfred Junge.
(Alfred Junge/© ITV/La Cinémathèque française)

Above: Production design for the schoolroom in *Black Narcissus* (1947) by Alfred Junge. (Alfred Junge/© ITV/BFI National Archive)

Right: Costume design for the Young General (Sabu) in *Black Narcissus* (1947) by Hein Heckroth (Hein Heckroth/© ITV/ BFI National Archive)

Production design for the schoolroom in *Black Narcissus* (1947) by Alfred Junge. (Alfred Junge/© ITV/ BFI National Archive)

Storyboard drawings for *Black Narcissus* (1947) by Ivor Beddoes. (Ivor Beddoes/© ITV/ BFI National Archive)

Poster for *The Tales of Hoffmann* (1951) by Marc Stone. The poster was one of three different designs that referenced the film's structuring around distinct colour schemes. (Marc Stone/BFI National Archive)

Production design for Venice, Act 2, in *The Tales of Hoffmann* (1951) by Ivor Beddoes. (Ivor Beddoes/ ©STUDIOCANAL/BFI National Archive)

Production design for Act 3, *The Tales of Hoffmann* (1951) by Ivor Beddoes. (Ivor Beddoes/ ©STUDIOCANAL/BFI National Archive)

Production design for epilogue, *The Tales of Hoffmann* (1951) by Ivor Beddoes. (Ivor Beddoes/ ©STUDIOCANAL/BFI National Archive)

Act 3, *The Tales of Hoffmann* (1951). (©STUDIOCANAL)

Production design for Act 3, *The Tales of Hoffmann* (1951) by Ivor Beddoes. (Ivor Beddoes/
©STUDIOCANAL/BFI National Archive)

Production design for *Gone to Earth* (1950) by Ivor Beddoes. (Ivor Beddoes/©Disney/
BFI National Archive)

Notes from a Costume Designer

Sandy Powell

Watching Powell and Pressburger's films again – *A Matter of Life and Death* (1946), *The Red Shoes* (1948), *Black Narcissus* (1947), *I Know Where I'm Going!* (1945), *Tales of Hoffmann* (1951), *Peeping Tom* (1960) – I recognise my own work in all of them. Even if it's unconscious, the references are there. And it's not simply my own work, but that of so many others. You can see just how much they've done to inspire filmmakers working today.

There are two things that stand out to me. The first is the way in which costume design, production design and lighting all work together, as a whole. Hein Heckroth did both the costumes and the art direction for some productions, and you can really tell. It all comes together, as theatre does. That's the second point. You can absolutely see that these people have come from the theatre. There's a theatricality to it all, even in the works that are realistic. That's also what I brought to film, a sensibility from my time in the theatre. It's where I started out, studying theatre design at art school before working with [dancer and choreographer] Lindsay Kemp. I went straight into haute theatricality! And when I revisit *Tales of Hoffmann* and *The Red Shoes*, there's so much of Lindsay there: small bits of choreography that I recognise; the settings and design. Looking back, I can see that he was inspired by Powell and Pressburger. And because all of my own work comes back to Lindsay, I've been inspired without even realising it. It's come through the people that I've worked with.

I love colour. For me it's the most important thing, and often it's the first thing I think of when I'm designing. When I'm imagining a character and how they're going to look,

Costume design for Carol Aird (Cate Blanchett) in *Carol* (2015) by Sandy Powell.
(© Sandy Powell/Collection of the artist)

Cate Blanchett as Carol Aird in *Carol* (2015), photographed by Wilson Webb. (© Studiocanal Ltd.)

quite often I'll get a feeling of a colour before I even have a shape or an item of cloth-ing in mind. Sometimes I see characters in colour; other times it's scenes that I see. It's instinctive. And I want to have an idea of how colour will work across the production, particularly the locations.

You can see that colour is very important to Powell and Pressburger, too. I enjoy the whites in *Black Narcissus*, because it's not just one shade. The white is in layers. Lots of creams and off whites in different textures. It's beautiful because it has such depth, and it's very painterly. The thing I'm personally very careful with is the use of red, because it's symbolic. But I also love red when it is used properly. *Black Narcissus* uses red in this very specific way. When Sister Ruth (Kathleen Byron) wears the red dress, it's not a bright scarlet but a deep, dark red. But when she puts on the lipstick it's that pure red which is so symbolic, and so striking, in the middle of that landscape with its pale, neutral tones. Amongst the habits, that red is so defiant and so brilliant. In *The Red Shoes*, the incredible thing is that there isn't really any red apart from in the shoes themselves. That's why it works. And in Powell's *Peeping Tom*, Helen Stephens (Anna Massey) is in a coral red dress before she goes into the dark room, and there's that red light. Red for danger.

Costume design for Therese Belivet (Rooney Mara) in *Carol* (Todd Haynes, 2015) by Sandy Powell. (Sandy Powell/ ©Number 9 Films, Channel 4/Collection of the artist)

A celestial vantage point in *A Matter of Life and Death* (1946) photographed by Eric Gray. (Eric Gray/© ITV/ BFI National Archive)

6

Metaphors of Vision

Ian Christie

Imagine an eye unruled by man-made laws of perspective, an eye unprejudiced by compositional logic, an eye which does not respond to the name of everything but which must know each object encountered in life through an adventure of perception.

Stan Brakhage, *Metaphors on Vision*[1]

In 1971, Michael Powell began to write what he called 'a long novel about the movie business', which would be an autobiography told with some fictional freedom. The title was to be 'I'm an Eye', and after setting the scene in an editing room at night, where the narrator is left alone to ruminate, there is a remarkable hymn to the power of the image:

I'm an eye.

I'm today's sunset and tomorrow's sunrise

I'm that face in the crowd, the texture of that tree, the pattern of the pavement.

I'm Matisse.

I'm Daumier, Sidney Paget, Bruce Bairnsfather, Low, Giles

I'm Giacometti, Rodin, Maillol, Isamu Noguchi, Frank Lloyd Wright

I'm Bosch

I'm an eye.

---

1. Stan Brakhage, *Metaphors of Vision*, in *Film Culture* 30 (Autumn 1963), 25. The opening lines of *Metaphors of Vision*, an important manifesto by the American avant-garde filmmaker Stan Brakhage (republished in 2017, New York: Light Industry), containing his challenge to think beyond the apparent limitations of 'the camera eye'. Brakhage's work was probably unknown to Powell, but would no doubt have struck a common chord.

As this train of thought becomes more frankly autobiographical, Powell offers a kaleidoscopic sequence of images recalled from his own films – 'I carry them all in my head' – and memories of great early filmmakers, before reaching back even further to the great illustrators of the Victorian and Edwardian period that shaped his early imagination.

This seems to have been an attempt to explain what he had expressed more cryptically in what has become a famous 1968 interview with Bertrand Tavernier focused on *Peeping Tom*:

> Most directors of my generation have their own style, but I don't… *I live cinema*. I chose the cinema when I was very young, sixteen years old, and from this time on, my memories almost coincide with the history of the cinema… *I am the cinema*. I grew up with and through the cinema; if I interested myself in pictures, books or music, it is again thanks to the cinema.[2]

Powell was trying to convey his sense of belonging to a tradition of image-making and visual storytelling that stretched back far beyond the span of cinema itself. Eventually he would embark on the magnificent two-volume autobiography that we have.[3] But I think there is something vital and immediate captured in the earlier exercise in self-examination, which seems to take us to the heart of Powell's relationship to cinema.

Is there any way to explain this? Powell himself would write in his second volume of memoir that 'the craft is a mystery…nobody can explain it', adding that he felt like 'a high priest of the mysteries', taking his authority for granted.[4] Perhaps the clearest vindication of this attitude is found in what was Powell's own favourite among his films, *A Matter of Life and Death* (1946). In this belated war film, conceived during World War Two, but made and released after it, the issues at stake are at once national, international and cosmic. And they are focused in the central figure of an English village doctor, who turns out to be also a respected neurologist and ultimately a persuasive 'spokesman for Britain' in the film's great celestial trial. However, we first meet him surveying his rural domain through the historic device of a camera obscura (see design, opposite), which he explains to his visitor, an American radio operator, allows him to 'see it all clearly, and at once, as in a poet's eye' – a phrase that might stand for the Archers' lasting appeal. The camera obscura is by no means the most spectacular apparatus in this film, which includes a neurological operating theatre and a giant escalator linking heaven and earth, like a modernised version of the biblical

---

2.   Powell quoted in *Michael Powell: Interviews* ed. David Lazar (Jackson: University Press of Mississippi, 2003), 29. Translated from an interview with Bertrand Tavernier and Jacques Prayer in *Midi-Minuit Fantastique*.

3.   Michael Powell, *A Life in Movies* (London: Heinemann, 1986); Michael Powell, *Million-Dollar Movie* (London: Heinemann, 1992).

4.   Powell, *Million-Dollar Movie*, 16.

Production design for the camera obscura in *A Matter of Life and Death* (1946) by Alfred Junge. (Alfred Junge/ ©ITV/The Harry Ransom Center)

Jacob's Ladder.[5] Nor do we know which of the film's creators conceived this extraordinarily suggestive metaphor for filmic vision. But we can relate it to Powell's own account of his relationship with Pressburger: 'he always saw the whole thing at one moment; I often had to discover it'.[6] Whatever the empirical process of invention that lay behind these metaphysical images, which was no doubt collaborative, they are woven into a multi-layered meditation on what 'Britishness' stood for in the mid-twentieth century that mobilises Elizabethan poetry alongside modern technology.[7]

---

5. Genesis, 28: 10–19. Jacob dreams of a ladder linking heaven and earth.

6. Powell quoted on *The South Bank Show* (1986), Season 10, Episode 4, dir. David Hinton, ITV, 26 October.

7. On the orchestration of English cultural themes in the film, see: Ian Christie, *A Matter of Life and Death*, (London: British Film Institute, 2000).

Right: The Stairway to Heaven, nicknamed 'Ethel' by the crew, for *A Matter of Life and Death* (1946). Photographed by Eric Gray. (Eric Gray/© ITV/BFI National Archive)

Below: Production design for the Stairway to Heaven in *A Matter of Life and Death* (1946) by Alfred Junge. (Alfred Junge/© ITV/ La Cinémathèque française)

The elliptical image of the village street on Dr Reeves' antique camera obscura (one of which can still be found beside Edinburgh Castle) rhymes visually with an earlier image in the film, when dead airmen newly arrived in heaven's waiting room look down through a large circular opening onto the serried ranks of the celestial bureaucracy. And later, as the injured poet-pilot Peter Carter is anaesthetised for an operation, a veiny eyelid closing takes us 'inside' his mind (see p. 152), before we see the vast amphitheatre where his, and Britain's, 'case' will be tried.

The concentration of what I'm calling 'metaphors of vision' in *A Matter of Life and Death* may be exceptional, but similar motifs run through many of Powell's and Pressburger's films, both those they made together as the Archers and separately. These are images and moments that remind us we're watching a mediated form of seeing, which is cinema itself. In *A Canterbury Tale* (1944), another villager who is not what he appears, the gentleman farmer Thomas Colpeper, offers service personnel stationed near Canterbury a Magic Lantern lecture about the history of the old Pilgrim's Way.[8] Neither they nor we get to see his slides on-screen, but the blackout needed for the lecture creates a chiaroscuro effect as he speaks about the ancient pilgrims 'coming to Canterbury to ask for a blessing or to do penance'.

'Jacob's Ladder' or 'Jacob's Dream', 1799–1807, by William Blake, which served as an inspiration for *A Matter of Life and Death* (1946). (British Museum)

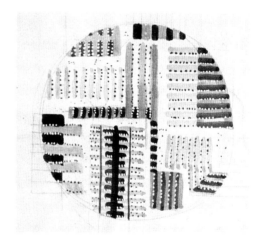

Production designs for the celestial vantage points in *A Matter of Life and Death* (1946) by Alfred Junge. (Alfred Junge/© ITV/La Cinémathèque française)

---

8.   On the ambivalence of the Colpeper figure, see: Ian Christie, 'History is Now and England: *A Canterbury Tale* in its contexts', in *The Cinema of Michael Powell: International Perspectives on an English Filmmaker*, (eds) Ian Christie and Andrew Moor (London: British Film Institute, 2005), 75–93.

Production design for Colpeper's Magic Lantern show in *A Canterbury Tale* (1944) by Alfred Junge. (Alfred Junge/ ©ITV/La Cinémathèque française)

Faced with sceptical questioning about the relevance of this history, Colpeper evokes the idea that these new pilgrims are seeing the same sights and hearing the same sounds as their ancestors. As the camera closes in on Eric Portman, with music underscoring his evocation, both the onscreen audience and we are briefly seduced into his vision – one that we've already experienced as costume drama in the film's opening scene of Chaucer's pilgrims.

Later in the Archers' canon there will be a range of devices in *The Red Shoes* (1948) to remind us of the contrast between audience's and performers' points of view: powerful spotlights picking out key moments of performance; Massine looking at the audience through a peephole in the curtain before the first night of the *Red Shoes* ballet; the mirrors in Vicky's final dressing room that multiply images of her impossible choices. Much of the film's magic depends on its ability to situate us, its audience, 'within' performances. And central to its successor, *The Tales of Hoffmann* (1951), is the capacity of that film's poet-hero for self-delusion in his romantic passions. The most extreme of these is for the inventor Coppélius' mechanical doll Olympia, danced by Moira Shearer, who only seems vibrantly real for him and us when he wears magic spectacles – a nineteenth-century dramatic device that we can perhaps better appreciate in the era of mobile apps and augmented reality.

Separately, Powell and Pressburger were both clearly drawn to scenarios that destabilise the security of the viewer watching a self-contained world on screen. One of Pressburger's feature-length successes in the mid-thirties, before meeting Powell, was an original story that actually begins in the cinema, with an actor mistakenly kissing a stranger in the dark instead of the woman he's meeting clandestinely, filmed first in Paris and later re-made in Hollywood as *One Rainy Afternoon* (1936).[9] As the scandal grows, boosted by a sensation-hungry press, the film plays with different levels of 'reality' before coming full circle to end in an auditorium. Pressburger's last film in France would also look forward to some of the Archers' radical time-shifts. Taking its title from Jacques Offenbach's operetta

Hoffmann (Robert Rounseville) wearing the magic spectacles he acquires from Coppélius, *The Tales of Hoffmann* (1951). (©STUDIOCANAL/BFI National Archive)

9. *Monsieur Sans-Gêne* (Karl Anton, France, 1935); *One Rainy Afternoon* (Rowland V. Lee,, USA, 1937).

La vie parisienne, this starts in the Paris of the 1900 Exposition Universelle before flashing forward to 1936, when a Brazilian millionaire returns to the scene of his early love-affair, ready to be re-enchanted by Paris. Kevin Macdonald, Pressburger's grandson, admires how his grandfather's script poetically described the crucial time-slip:

> It was exactly midnight and very quietly the clock began to chime a little melody. When it stopped, Fernando went on hearing it, chiming through the years and decades of his life.[10]

From what is known of his early German and French careers, there seems little doubt that Pressburger brought to the Archers' partnership a sophisticated narrative imagination, which Powell was ready to translate into concretely realised metaphors. Early drafts of the *A Matter of Life and Death* script apparently called for elaborate ghostly apparitions, yet in the final film, the metaphysical structure is made literal by the relatively simple devices of heaven 'freezing' earthly action, and the stairway connecting the two cheekily updated as a giant escalator.

The pair did not abandon their early fascination with exploiting filmic vision and its analogues in later projects. In 1952, Pressburger developed an Archers' script about the life of the composer Richard Strauss, *The Golden Years*, which would have been played entirely to a subjective camera, with Strauss himself appearing only in a home-movie fragment at the end. Despite the relative success of the equally stylised *Tales of Hoffmann*, this did not find backing. But traces of the idea survive in their *Oh... Rosalinda!!* (1955), an updated version of Johann Strauss's operetta *Die Fledermaus*, with Anton Walbrook opening the film by directly addressing the camera to invite the audience into the raffish world of post-war Vienna. By the time of their last collaboration, television was an inescapable feature of everyday life. And in *The Boy Who Turned Yellow*, made for the Children's Film Foundation in 1972, the etymology of this 'far seeing' device may have suggested it as a portal for the young hero to pay a nocturnal visit to the Tower of London.[11] This low-budget comedy can hardly compare with the splendour of Powell's introduction to high-level fantasy with *The Thief of Bagdad* (1940), but the schoolboy's guide 'Nick', an electronic sprite emerging from the family TV set, is surely a descendent of that film's towering Djinn, and indeed of *A Matter of Life and Death*'s mercurial Conductor 71.

---

10. Kevin Macdonald, *Emeric Pressburger: the Life and Death of a Screenwriter* (London: Faber and Faber, 1994), 117.

11. The etymology of 'television' is based on 'seeing from a distance', as is the German *Fernsehen*.

The cast of *Oh... Rosalinda!!* (1955), photographed by Ronnie Pilgrim. (Ronnie Pilgrim/© STUDIOCANAL/ BFI National Archive)

Powell's own use of filmic self-reference would reach a climax with *Peeping Tom* in 1960, from a script by the former code-breaker turned screenwriter Leo Marks. Much of the scandal that this originally provoked may have been due to a mounting moral panic over supposed depravity in popular media during the 1950s.[12] But for later audiences *Peeping Tom* has become a rich parable about the nature of cinema itself. The film's opening, set in a nocturnal London alley, makes the audience an accomplice to a gruesome experiment in terror, with the camera itself seemingly a lethal weapon. In what follows, we're drawn into a young cameraman's relentless mission to complete his gruesome documentary with further elaborately staged murders. One of these takes place after hours at a large film studio (actually Pinewood, where Powell had often worked), where Mark is employed as a camera assistant shooting anodyne thrillers, and another in the sleazy Soho studio where he works

---

12. The 1950s saw a popular campaign mounted against 'horror comics', and *Peeping Tom* (1960) appeared amid a wave of films promising 'horrific' content, such as *The Stranglers of Bombay* (1959), *The Brain Eaters* (1958) and *Circus of Horrors* (1960). See also, Ian Christie, 'The Scandal of *Peeping Tom*', in *Powell, Pressburger and Others*, ed. Christie (London: British Film Institute, 1978), 53–59.

Production design for *Peeping Tom* (1960) by Ivor Beddoes. (Ivor Beddoes/©STUDIOCANAL/BFI National Archive)

part-time producing pornographic pictures. These two poles of commercial filmmaking serve to frame his 'amateur' obsession with exorcising the memory of being filmed as a child by his father.

'All this filming isn't healthy', declares the mother of a girl who has befriended him, herself blind, but aware that strange things are afoot in the attic studio above her. For Mark, filming is indeed a compulsion, an illness; and a psychiatrist, invited to the film studio after Mark's second murder, translates his mention of 'what makes people Peeping Toms' into the psychiatric term scoptophilia, 'the morbid urge to gaze'. Mark, we are to understand, has been traumatised by his father's experiments in filming him reacting to

a range of morbid subjects, which we see as home-movie footage, with the father played by Michael Powell himself and the young Mark by Powell's own son Columba, giving the story a teasing personal dimension.

In fact, the original script embroidered its theme with more detail. When Helen strikes up a tentative relationship with Mark, she tells him that the idea for her children's book, *The Magic Camera*, came from seeing him leave home clutching his camera every day.[13] Her magic camera belongs to a young boy who is terrified of adults and it shows grown-ups as if they were children, which distantly recalls Pressburger's script for *I'd Rather Have Cod Liver*

---

13. *Peeping Tom*. Faber Classic Screenplay Series (London: Faber, 1998), 138. The provenance of this text is unclear, but it includes dialogue not used in the film, likely to come from a pre-production screenplay.

Oil (1931), the short that was Max Ophüls' debut as a filmmaker.[14] But it primarily counterpoints Mark's photographing erotic subjects, which he also wants to kill, in a vain effort to exorcise his early trauma. The unexpected casting of the Austrian actor Carl Boehm as Mark gave the film's central character an unexpected gravity, more in the tradition of Edgar Allan Poe's Roderick Usher or Villiers de l'Isle Adam's Axel than a typical young Londoner of the Sixties.[15] And despite the knowing comedy of the film studio and the Soho newsagent scenes, with their puns and *doubles entendres* about seeing, the intensity of the murders and Mark's solitary obsession create a sense of cinema itself being unhealthily voyeuristic. This idea has been reinforced by one of the film's leading admirers, Martin Scorsese, linking it with the making of his own *Taxi Driver* (1976), another film about a lonely obsessive.[16]

The best analysis of how the film's climax might be interpreted psychoanalytically has been offered by Laura Mulvey:

> Mark's suicide is also a murder. The sadist is released into masochism. The victim's gaze will turn on the male voyeur and finally succeed in turning the all-seeing father into its object. Mark will then be able to 'kill the father by killing himself... We see Mark's suicide figured doubly as a death drive: a drive to his end and to the end of the story. The spectacle of his death balances and retrospectively transforms the opening spectacle of Dora's murder.[17]

Mulvey draws attention to the importance of the actual devices involved in *Peeping Tom*: the 16mm camera that Mark wields, the still cameras wired to trigger in succession, like a modern recapitulation of Eadweard Muybridge's famous photographs of a horse galloping, one of the avatars of cinema. Earlier, the critic Raymond Durgnat, one of Powell's earliest supporters, published a study of its 'image cluster' – 'eye/camera/ mirror/bayonet' and the paradoxical equation between blindness and insight represented by Helen's mother.[18]

Of all Powell's late unrealised projects, his long-cherished adaptation of Shakespeare's *The Tempest* promised most in its conceptual ambition. First mooted in 1969, after he had made *Age of Consent* (Michael Powell, 1969) in Australia, and initially with the backing of

---

14. Macdonald, *Emeric Pressburger*, 76–81.

15. Laura Mulvey, 'The Light That Failed', *The Cinema of Michael Powell: International Perspectives on an English Filmmaker*, (eds) Ian Christie and Andrew Moor (London: British Film Institute, 2005), 148. Mulvey describes Mark as 'like a Romantic artist reaching out... in a perverted search for the Sublime'.

16. *Scorsese on Scorsese*, ed Ian Christie and David Thompson (London: Faber, 2003), 20.

17. Mulvey, 'The Light That Failed', *The Cinema of Michael Powell*, 155.

18. Raymond Durgnat, 'Movie crazy, or the man(iac) with the movie camera', *Framework*, no. 9, Winter 1978–9, 3.

Production design for *The Tempest*, unrealised, c. 1970–72, by Ivor Beddoes. (© Ivor Beddoes/BFI National Archive)

that film's star and co-producer James Mason, this project changed location and personnel frequently during the following years. In some ways, *Age of Consent* can be seen to contain the germ of Powell's *Tempest*, with its dissatisfied ageing artist retreating to a remote island setting, where a process of renewal can start. However, Powell's *Magic Island* was to be 'completely un-naturalistic' with 'everything a studio set or a painting', and his Prospero,

> a Renaissance man, not… the Wizard of Oz. He and Galileo, his contemporary, are the
> heirs of Leonardo Da Vinci and Amerigo Vespucci. My island is not a Mediterranean
> *plage*… it is a creation of the Reformation, an intellectual concept.[19]

This vision of Shakespeare owed much to the critic Jan Kott's influential 1964 book *Shakespeare Our Contemporary*, although Kott had declared 'Prospero's island has nothing in common with the happy isles of Renaissance Utopias'.[20] Instead, he invoked 'the world of the late Gothics' and specifically 'the mad Hieronymous Bosch', 'precursor of the Baroque and Surrealism', with the teeming world of his *Garden of Earthly Delights* (1500) as a model for the 'cruel tortures' of Shakespeare's island.

19.   Quoted in Ian Christie, *Arrows of Desire: The Films of Michael Powell and Emeric Pressburger* (London: Faber, 1994), 108.

20.   Jan Kott, *Shakespeare Our Contemporary* (London: Methuen, 1964), 188.

Powell would retain Bosch as one visual source for his island, complementing this with Goya's painting *The Colossus* (1808), with its giant towering above a landscape of diminutive figures, which, as Judith Buchanan observes, 'reinforces the sense of Prospero functioning in an entirely different dimension from the other creatures on his island'.[21] But it was also important for Powell to establish a different frame of reference, which led him to write his own prologue for the play, in which Prospero converses with Galileo beside a telescope before his banishment. They reject the church's power 'to deny the natural laws with Papal Bulls', insisting 'these lenses set men free!'.[22] Intellectually free, perhaps, but as Powell conceived Prospero's domination over his place of exile, the island would be tantamount to a police state, with elaborate surveillance:

> Prospero's cell is, in Powell's treatment of the play, inside a giant skull in the side of the mountain. Prospero never leaves his skull-cell, relying on the agency of Ariel and Caliban whenever he wishes to intervene in the world beyond.[23]

Buchanan compares this arrangement with Francis Walsingham's 'infamous secret service' network of spies within the Elizabethan state, describing the Skull as a 'command and control centre' which gives both Prospero and potential spectators of the film 'direct access to action and dialogue as it is taking place elsewhere'. She also refers intriguingly to an Elizabethan stage precedent, in Robert Greene's play *Friar Bacon and Friar Bungay* (1594), when 'a prospective glass' was used to enable 'the scene of the observer and that of the observed to be played out simultaneously', despite being set some miles apart.[24] But what Powell conceived in his notes to the *Magic Island* script suggests some kind of anthropomorphic sculpture, with the cartoonist and illustrator Gerald Scarfe involved in its preliminary design:

> The two great EYE-SOCKETS look out over the island. The EAR-CAVITIES are wired for sound. The cavernous MOUTH is CALIBAN'S LAIR... There are strange machines with cords, wheels and pulleys, one of them 25 feet high. There are cranes, weights, and

---

21.   The fullest published study of Powell's project is: Judith Buchanan, '"Like this insubstantial pageant faded": Michael Powell's *The Tempest*', *Film Studies* no. 2, Spring 2000, 85.

22.   *Tempest* script. Powell Papers This prelude was performed and filmed by David Thompson as part of his *Late Show Special* on Powell, BBC Television, 1992.

23.   Buchanan, 'Michael Powell's *The Tempest*', 87.

24.   Ibid, n.30, p. 90. A 'prospective glass' was an early form of telescope.

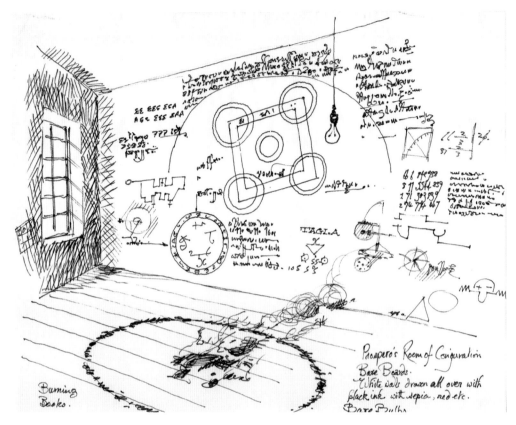

Drawing for 'Prospero's Room', *The Tempest* (Derek Jarman, 1979) by Christopher Hobbs. (Christopher Hobbs/© Kendon Films Ltd./BFI National Archive)

balances… Prospero's work-room occupies the whole of the **BRAIN-CAVITY**… from here Prospero controls the island. It is a power-house'.[25]

During his frustrated search for funding, Powell may have reflected that Ken Adam had designed and built a structure on this scale, although in a very different context, for the fifth Bond production, *You Only Live Twice* (1967). Created at Pinewood, Blofeld's vast headquarters is supposedly concealed inside an extinct volcano. However, Powell would no doubt also have recalled with some nostalgia the celestial apparatus at his disposal just twenty years earlier for *A Matter of Life and Death*.[26]

---

25. Quoted in Buchanan, 87.

26. On Powell's search for financing for *The Magic Island*, see *Million-Dollar Movie* (London: Heinemann, 1992), 515–21.

Although Powell failed to find backing for his vision of *The Tempest* in the filmmaking climate of the 1960s and 70s, his belief that Shakespeare's play could support radical film adaptation was vindicated by the new generation of Britain's independent filmmakers. In 1979, Derek Jarman would realise his own version of *The Tempest*, in which the play becomes essentially a dream of revenge hatched by the exiled Prospero. And in 1991, Peter Greenaway's *Prospero's Books* located the play entirely within its central character's imagination, encapsulating a wide range of other media – mime, dance, opera and animation – as well as art-historical references. Neither of these alluded directly to Powell's conception, although Jarman, as an Archers' admirer, said that he felt he had 'inherited' it from Powell, but in their different ways both vindicated the idea of an 'island of the mind'.[27]

The great Russian director Sergei Eisenstein, just seven years older than Powell, also believed that cinema was the culmination of many earlier forms of art and visual communication. And during the 1940s, when the Archers were creating their masterpieces, Eisenstein was pouring everything he knew into what would be his final film, *Ivan the Terrible* (1944), while also trying to explain in his parallel theoretical writings how cinema synthesised all the arts that preceded it.[28] One of his last essays was on the promise of 'stereo-cinema', which he saw as the culmination of a long history of trying to break down the 'fourth wall' between performance and spectator. And among many examples of tactics to achieve this in cinema, Eisenstein picked out two recent cases that had evidently impressed him: the climax of Hitchcock's *Spellbound* (1945) and Peter's 'going under' anaesthetic in *A Matter of Life and Death*, both described in scrupulous detail.[29]

Writing at a time when Stalin's campaign against 'cosmopolitanism' was at his height, there is what feels like a dutiful denunciation of these as examples of the 'pathological introspection' of artists working under capitalism. But reading Eisenstein today, as his long-censored writings circulate, we can sense his aesthetic excitement at discovering contemporary films that were free to explore such immersive strategies. And significantly, if perhaps surprisingly, both of these great filmmakers were staunch admirers of Walt Disney, relishing

---

27. On Jarman's relationship to Powell, see: Christie, *Arrows of Desire*, 99.

28. Eisenstein's unfinished text *Method* has recently been edited and published in part in English translation in two volumes: *Sergei Eisenstein: Disney* and *The Primal Phenomenon: Art* (Berlin: Potemkin Press, 2013, 2017), (eds) Oksana Bulgakowa & Dietmar Hochmuth, trans. Dustin Condren.

29. Sergei Eisenstein, 'On Stereo-cinema' (1947), (trans.) Sergey Levchin, *Public* 47, '3D Cinema and Beyond' , 2013. The wartime alliance between the USSR and Britain and America had enabled many Western films to enter Russia, which presumably accounts for Eisenstein having unexpected access to recent American, and British films.

Production design for *Spellbound*
(Alfred Hitchcock, 1945) by an
unknown sketch artist, after a
concept by Salvador Dalí.
(© Disney/BFI National Archive)

their friendships with the maestro of wholly invented filmic worlds in his animation. Both had also looked beyond the confines of the cinema apparatus in the mid-forties, imagining a future in which cinema could become the true successor of earlier arts.[30]

Today, thanks to the ongoing work of restoration and digital diffusion, Powell's and Pressburger's work is more widely available than it ever was during their lifetimes. Films that were impossible to see for decades now disclose their carefully crafted secrets and sub-texts as well as their visual and dramatic splendour, and continue to find new audiences. We know much more about Powell's attitudes and career, although Pressburger, like his partner, had little taste for analysing their work, preferring to speak obliquely of coaxing 'a little bit of magic' into 'cosy nests' in one of his rare public appearances.[31] But he too remained fascinated by the paradoxes of vision, and among his unrealised projects was the adaptation of an autobiographical novel by the blind Danish writer Karl Bjarnhof that told of the slow fading of sight. It ends with the narrator imagining he is answering an invisible child's question: 'I try a little magic trick I know; I try to make it sound like a fairy tale'.[32]

---

30. On Powell's commitment to realising the immersive potential of cinema, see: Ian Christie, 'Dying for Art: Michael Powell's Journey towards Duke Bluebeard's Castle and the Filmic Art-work of the Future', *Bluebeard's Legacy: death and secrets from Bartok to Hitchcock*, (eds) Griselda Pollock and Victoria Anderson, (London: I. B. Tauris, 2009), 175–199.

31. Pressburger introducing *A Canterbury Tale* at the Museum of Modern Art in 1980, quoted in Macdonald, *Emeric Pressburger*, 240.

32. Karl Bjarnhof, *The Good Light*, trans. Naomi Walford (London: Methuen, 1960), 264. This was the second of two autobiographical novels by Bjarnhof that Pressburger considered promising for screen adaptation. Its predecessor, *The Stars Grow Pale* (1956), had attracted wide acclaim and may have been optioned by Pressburger.

Tracking shot away from HIGH COURT ——— MONOCHROME TO COLOUR.

Above and right:

Production designs for the celestial vantage points in *A Matter of Life and Death* (1946) by Alfred Junge. (Alfred Junge/© ITV/La Cinémathèque française)

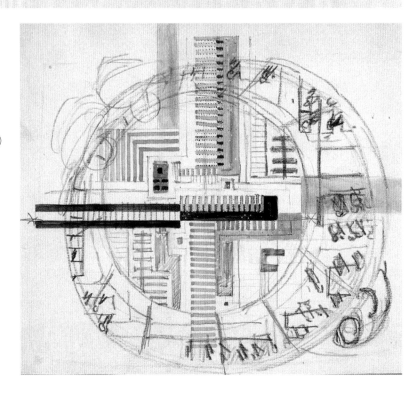

Above: Coppélius' magic spectacles. Original prop from *The Tales of Hoffmann* (1951) by Ivor Beddoes. (Ivor Beddoes/BFI National Archive)

Below and left: Coppélius' book. Original prop from *The Tales of Hoffmann* (1951) by Ivor Beddoes. (Ivor Beddoes/BFI National Archive)

147

Production design for *Oh… Rosalinda!!* (1955) by Hein Heckroth, showing alcohol-induced double vision. (Hein Heckroth/© STUDIOCANAL/Theaterwissenschaftliche Sammlung der Universität zu Köln)

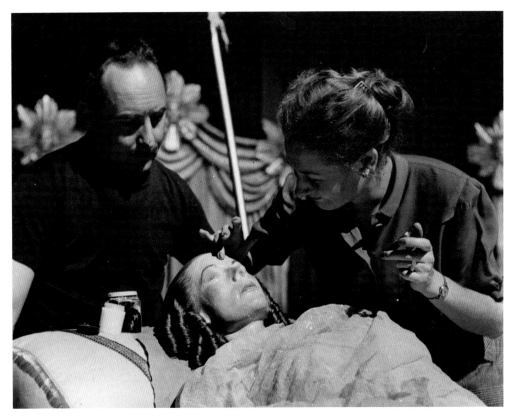

Assistant designer Ivor Beddoes and make-up artist Connie (Constance) Reeve at work on the mechanical doll, *The Tales of Hoffmann* (1951), photographed by Bert Cann. (Bert Cann/© STUDIOCANAL/BFI National Archive)

Above and below: Production designs for *Peeping Tom* (Michael Powell, 1960) by Ivor Beddoes. (Ivor Beddoes/ ©STUDIOCANAL/ BFI National Archive)

Above and below: Concept art for *Peeping Tom* (Michael Powell, 1960) by Ivor Beddoes. (Ivor Beddoes/ ©STUDIOCANAL/BFI National Archive)

Mark Lewis (Karlheinz Böhm as Carl Boehm) and his camera in *Peeping Tom* (Michael Powell, 1960) photographed by Norman Gryspeerdt. (Norman Gryspeerdt/© STUDIOCANAL/BFI National Archive)

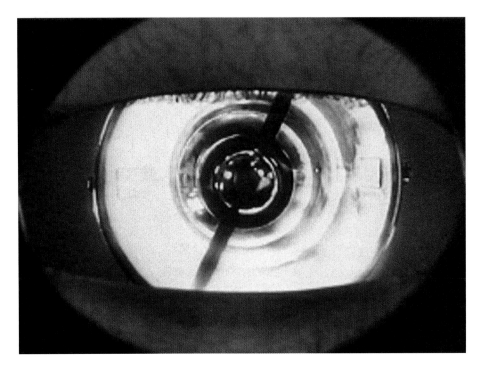

A Matter of Life and Death (1946). (© ITV)

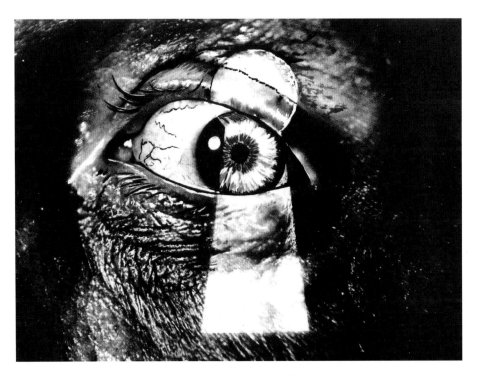

Looking through the keyhole in *Peeping Tom* (1960), photographed by Norman Gryspeerdt. This image was also used as the basis for the poster artwork. (Norman Gryspeerdt/© STUDIOCANAL/BFI National Archive)

Sept 11. Monday.   10

6.30 am call for the Pyramids. We were a little late. The sun had already risen when we presented up, and was already colouring the face of the Sphinx pale rose. There were traces of coloured paint on the huge cheekbones and the ears are two metres high. The nose broken by Napoleon's cannon pointed directly at the rising sun. We walked around the great paws and stared at the Great Pyramid rising into the sky. There is a tripod about 8 metres high on the blunt top to show the original height of the apex.

"One boy run up - down in eight minutes" announced the driver. "Only one. He know all the stones."

here is no mortar: each block is held + supported by another block.

"I took 15 seasons" said Khalil. "In the dry weather When the Nile flood all the people come here + work. When the waters go they go back to their farms and grow crops. Four months every year all the people of Egypt build the pyramid."

there are three huge pyramids and ten small ones in all discovered in the sand.

"I wish they would find a No. 14" grumbles Kamel. "My country might have better luck."

We walked all around the excavators + the cemetery, trying to find a natural feature on which one could construct a set. Nothing. We drove up the road beside the great Pyramid and around the other two into the desert beyond. It was dotted with shacks. I was beginning to get an idea but I said nothing. Khalil plunged over the stony sand with great energy but when we came back I said, "Let's drive back to Pyramid 3 and look at those little pyramids beside it." Khalil knew what I had in mind. We left the car + walked down to the three crumbling pyramids in a line below the big one. You could see the desert between them and the sand dropped away in a curve to the distance.

Suddenly I could see Caliban sitting on the top of the small pyramid. It was just like those lost pyramids in Yucatan. All it needed were trailing vines and strange vegetation or flowers. Perhaps some temple hills in the middle distance. Our island was taking shape. It was a piece of lost Atlantis. Why shouldn't it have pyramids? And Caliban the last of a great kingly line of people.

We raced over the sand in the shadow of the Pyramid of Mycerinus. We drove to the Mena House Hotel, a huge + splendid relic of the Victorian age, where every famous man has stayed. It's built of brick and faced of wood, with wooden balconies + windows and springles up the hill, 150 yards long. In its own way it is as impressive as the Pyramid of Cheops, which looms above it through the palm-trees. We had coffee.

A page from a diary kept by Michael Powell during a location scouting visit to Egypt for *The Tempest*, unrealised, 1972. Powell travelled with art director Wilfred Shingleton, recording locations, studios and local manufacturing. (Michael Powell/BFI National Archive)

Notes from a Director

Joanna Hogg

When I first saw Martin Scorsese's *New York, New York* (1977) at the age of 19, I don't believe I had seen any of Powell and Pressburger's films. Still, that may have been my first glimpse of their visionary film-making: a glimpse refracted through Scorsese, who did so much to revive interest in their work. I suspect that this is not uncommon. Anyone today who watches a Powell and Pressburger film for the first time will likely find it familiar, such was the reach of their influence. Their style got into the atmosphere; it was everywhere.

It wasn't long after seeing *New York, New York* that I did watch Powell and Pressburger's films for the first time. I connected instantly with their otherworldly visions: *Gone to Earth* (1950) – the spellbinding, heart-wrenching foxhunting scene; *A Canterbury Tale* (1944) – the mysterious glue man and the beauty of Kent, where I grew up; *The Tales of Hoffmann* (1951) – I loved the visual puns, the tails disappearing behind doors; and, of course, *The Red Shoes* (1948).

At film school, I worked under their influence, and I borrowed their language to help find my own. I hadn't yet digested the lessons of their films, and so the imprint of their style shows visibly in my graduation film: *Caprice* (1986). In that film, a young woman crosses, Alice-like, into the pages of the fashion magazine she reads obsessively. The world she finds there, a dream world saturated in colour, I could not have dreamt of had I not seen *The Tales of Hoffman* and *The Red Shoes*. I made the film on a sound stage at film school, using painted gauzes in the style of Hein Heckroth.

Caprice (1986), an unknown Tilda Swinton. (Joanna Hogg/© NFTS)

Even when I left film school to work in TV, an industry whose demands meant that I could not always draw freely on my influences, their films remained a presence in my life. There are sounds, images, and lines of dialogue from their films that are deeply ingrained in my everyday experience; they are part of my lifetime memory bank. Whenever I smell fried onions, I think I may be hallucinating, like Peter Carter in *A Matter of Life and Death*. Powell and Pressburger were the filmmakers who showed me how cinema can tap into our dreams.

I can find traces of Powell and Pressburger in all of my work, but it was while making *The Souvenir* (2019) that I revisited them most consciously. In that film, I draw on my film school days in the early 1980s, and I spent a lot of time thinking my way back into the atmosphere of that period. Inevitably, I thought my way back to Powell and Pressburger and the way I felt when I first encountered their work.

It wasn't only the visual influence I carried with me but also the spirit of their films. I'm always moved by the climactic scene of *The Red Shoes*. After Vicky falls in front of an ap-

Caprice (1986).
(Joanna Hogg/
©NFTS)

proaching train, the impresario Boris Lermontov announces that 'Miss Page is unable to dance tonight, nor indeed any other night'. The company performs *The Red Shoes* in spite of its star's death, casting a spotlight onto the stage where Vicky would have danced. In *The Souvenir*: when Julie's boyfriend Anthony dies (earlier, he had claimed to admire Powell & Pressburger in a bid to impress her) Julie has to find the resolve to carry on making films. I think of that moment as drawing on the spirit of *The Red Shoes*.

As I write this, I am about to enter production on a new film. Throughout the writing and development, *A Matter of Life and Death* has been on my mind. The influence of that film may appear directly only in one moment – a scene of flute-playing that recalls the young goatherd playing the flute in the sand dunes when Peter Carter emerges from his crash-landing – and yet indirectly, *A Matter of Life and Death* is in its fabric. That tends to be the way with the work of great artists like Powell and Pressburger: one remembers the specific moments – the smell of fried onions or a spotlight on an empty stage – but the lasting impact is a vision so bold and unique that it challenges you to make your own.

The Souvenir Part II (2021) photographed by Joss Barratt (top) and Agatha A Nitecka (above).
(Joss Barratt, Agatha Nitecka/©BBC, British Film Institute/BFI National Archive)BFI National Archive)

'The Red Shoes' from Hans Christian Andersen, *Fairy Tales*, 1924, illustrated by Kai Nielsen. (©British Library/ Bridgeman Images)

7

The Red Shoes

Marina Warner

Redness and shoes both belong to the primary lexicon of fairy tales, the offspring of the logic of the imaginary, which isn't exclusively verbal. As Michael Powell said, 'film is essentially visual',[1] and the visuals of fairy tale are couched in a primal, pre-verbal language written with the body, its limbs, nerves and internal organs, through movement, material qualities, texture, colour, sheen and sparkle. The Archers dazzlingly took up this legacy; their ambition of 'composed film' fused story, drama, music, movement (of the camera as well as the personae) and images. Furthermore, cinema could break through the manifest world to other worlds below, above, and beyond. The libretti of Romantic ballets frequently conjure another realm, haunted by the unquiet dead and ethereal creatures and demonic figures from pagan legends; in the Archers' film of *The Red Shoes* (1948), we glimpse *Giselle*, *Les Sylphides* and *Swan Lake*, all three classic works taking place in a twilit space contiguous to this world, made visible through dance; a passing scene from Coppelia also hints at automata and puppet masters. The filmmakers were intensely drawn to inhabiting these other worlds of imagination and created an original work, 'The Ballet of the Red Shoes', embedded at the heart of their film. Throughout, they explore, self-reflexively, the passions and processes that are necessary to achieve the spell of such spectacles, showing us from every angle how the piece came to be made, and returning to linger again and again on the shoes themselves, gleaming red like a polished apple or high gloss lipstick and trailing associations of warnings, blood, wounds, orifices.

---

1. *Michael Powell – A Life in Movie* [Radio], BBC Meridian, dir. Bryan Forbes, pres. Frank Delaney, 4 November 1986. Available online: https://www.bbc.co.uk/programmes/p03m0qfm

Relief with dancing Maenads by Callimachus, late 1st century BCE. (© Azoor Photo/Alamy Stock Photo)

The new medium of Technicolor handed them a lustrous super-saturated palette that enhances Moira Shearer's shining fall of red hair and pearly skin; and, with Brian Easdale's symphonic score, they are able to convey high voltage passion – and danger.

The fairytale symbol of the red shoes reverberates with several much-loved stories. The Cinderella cycle revolves around the lost slipper, and in 'Ashypet', the Grimm Brothers' version, the heroine's sisters are urged by their mother to cut off their heels and cut off their toes to fit into the glass slipper. When each of them in turn rides off with the prince, the doves warn him, 'Turn and peep, turn and peep,/There's blood within the shoe…' The evil queen at the end of 'Snow White' dances in red hot shoes till she drops down dead. In the story of 'The Shoes that Were Danced to Tatters' (also known as 'The Twelve Dancing Princesses'), the heroines wear out a pair of shoes every night and no one knows they have been meeting twelve princes and dancing till dawn. Interestingly, a Danish version features only one princess, who has twelve pairs of golden shoes, and she wears them out when she takes a boat each night to visit a troll to gallivant with him all night long.[2] Enchanted footwear – seven league boots, the Silver Shoes that Dorothy, in L. Frank Baum's book, clicks three times to travel to Oz and back again – can carry the wearer across to other world (Dorothy's were changed into the famous ruby slippers for the 1939 Hollywood film, *The Wizard of Oz*, and they cast a glowing shadow on the ballet pumps in the film of *The Red Shoes*, though these have a far less benign charge).

The fairy tale in its most famous version was written by Hans Christian Andersen and published in 1845; it and has enjoyed huge success ever since, inspiring artists and illustrators all over the world.[3] Andersen was born in 1805 on an island in the Baltic in the small Danish town of Odense in conditions of brutal poverty; his mother was a washerwoman and his grandmother worked in in the local asylum; neither of them was literate or altogether 'respectable'; his father and his stepfather were both cobblers, with many customers who stopped by to talk. Andersen's biographers have revealed how his own torments fed the morbid punishments and humiliations in his tales – by all accounts he was a peculiar, ungainly, unlovely figure, snobbish and chippy, beset by foibles and phobias, and tending to fall passionately in love with unobtainable men and women. Significantly he cross-genders the stories' points of identification: he projects himself as the mermaid, the match girl, and the girl who transgresses by loving her red shoes.

Andersen heard stories from his family and neighbours, and he was familiar with the Grimm Brothers' *Children's and Household Tales*, which first came out in 1812; he also knew the bizarre, alarming stories of E. T. A. Hoffman, the originator of the Coppelia story with his tale 'The Sandman', which inspired Freud to define the Uncanny – tales that aren't fit for the nursery at all. Andersen relates his in a light, breezy manner with complicit asides to his audience about human folly, but a streak of Victorian disapproval, not present in his predecessors, runs through his storytelling. In his most magical tales, however, such as 'The Snow Queen', love and courage triumph: Gerda valiantly overcomes ordeal after ordeal to reach Kai, and free him from the spell of the evil enchantress. The splinter of ice falls out of his eye as Gerda restores him to the human world of tenderness and roses.

Like thousands, no, millions of children, I loved Andersen's stories: the pious endings did not repel as they do now, and the mutilations (the little mermaid's tail split in two to

---

2. 'The Princess with the Twelve Pairs of Golden Shoes', *The Danish Fairy Book*, ed. Clara Stroebe, trans. Frederick H. Martens (New York: Frederick A. Stokes Company, 1922), 135–42. Digitised by the Internet Archive here: https://archive.org/details/danishfairybook00stro Accessed 4 June 2020.

3   See Jackie Wullschlager, 'Introduction', *The Fairy Tales of Hans Christian Andersen*, (ed.) Jackie Wullschlager, (trans.) Tiina Nunnally (London: Penguin, 2004).

Moira Shearer as Victoria Page in *The Red Shoes* (1948). (©ITV)

make her human legs; Karen's stumps and replacement wooden feet) excited a kind of perverse glee. But many adults now like myself find that Andersen's mawkish piety, his mixture of sado-masochism and jocosity, and his moralizing gender expectations seep into his stories, leaving an unpleasant taste.

And yet. And yet. The story he created inspired the Archers' unparalleled film.

'The Red Shoes' is one of Andersen's laconic cautionary fables, delivered in the deadpan style the Grimms are best known for. It is only a few pages long and a muddle, except for – and this is key – the decisive dance of death leading to Karen's apotheosis.[4] Karen, a 'delicate and charming' young girl, goes barefoot in summer and in winter has to wear clogs which turn her ankles red – the first entry of the colour into the story. Later, red shoes appear again and again, changing from marks of shameful poverty, signs of luxury, to sinful fetters.

The hue-family of reds to purples is associated at one end of the spectrum with pleasure, frivolity, luxury and sin, and no colour more so than scarlet ('a scarlet woman', *The Scarlet Letter*, Scarlett O'Hara ...). At the other they proclaim splendour, power and pres-

---

4.   *The Fairy Tales of Hans Christian Andersen*, (ed.) Jackie Wullschlager, (trans.) Tiina Nunnally, 207–212.

tige (the red carpet, cardinals' crimson robes, the Red Army). Michel Pastoureau, the preeminent historian of colour, comments that 'Red is colour incarnate... Formerly considered masculine, and strongly linked to power and war, red gradually became a feminine colour, a symbol of love and pleasure.' [5]

Karen wants all these connotations of redness: she's fatally attracted to luxury (a word which originates in the Latin word for Lust, *Luxuria*). When Karen goes to church, wearing the forbidden red shoes, an old soldier with a devilish long red beard leaning on a crutch by the door asks to wipe Karen's shoe, and when 'she stretched out her little foot... he slapped his hand on the soles' and says, 'Stay on tight when you dance!'[6]

The veteran's words are a prophecy and a curse, and from this moment the shoes control her and the fairy tale gathers pace. Her foster mother has fallen ill, but Karen still wants to go to the great ball in town – and is away when the old woman dies. Like so many of the uncanny animate things in Andersen's tales, the red shoes have a mind of their own and they carry off the wicked girl. Karen meets an angel, who spells out the curse: 'Dance from door to door. And wherever proud and vain children lie, you will knock so they hear and fear you! Dance you shall, dance!—'.

In her frenzy, Karen dances to the executioner's house and asks him not to cut off her head, as she shan't be able to repent if she has no head. Instead, he must cut off her feet. He makes her wooden feet; meanwhile the red shoes, with her severed feet still in them, keep on dancing across the fields and into the deep forest.

The Archers' film of *The Red Shoes* plunges Andersen's fairy tale into a hall of mirrors, in which the mythic story is refracted twice: the frame dramatises the conflict between the rising star Vicky Page (Moira Shearer) and the impresario-cum-puppet master Boris Lermontov (consummately silky and seductive Anton Walbrook), and her romance with the composer Julian Craster (Marius Goring). This plot is obliquely reprised, doubled and transformed in the ballet-within-the-film, which, at almost twenty minutes long, is a complete and original work in itself (a whole ballet company was created to bring it into being in a pioneering example of the new hybrid form, dance-cinema).

The figures in the film are also shadowed by the famous real-life history of the Ballets Russes, and Diaghilev's love affair with Vaslav Nijinsky. Surviving drawings and photographs of Nijinsky capture his androgynous grace and beauty – it wasn't a stretch to model

---

5. Michel Pastoureau, *Chroma* (London: Thames and Hudson, 2010), 15.

6. The old woman, Karen's patron, gives him a coin for his pains – in utter contradiction of her previous opposition to the shoes. This is one of the many inconsistencies in the story as written.

Vaslav Nijinsky in *Schéhérazade*, 1911,
photographed by Auguste Bert.
(National Portrait Gallery)

a female dancer on his persona. The way Diaghilev threw Nijinsky out of the company after he learned of the young dancer/choreographer's sudden marriage to Romola de Pulszky clearly inspired Pressburger's screenplay: Lermontov, on hearing of their love affair, brutally casts out Julian and Vicky.[7]

Among these memories glimpsed in the recesses of the mirrors, ghost presences closer in time also gather: the movie mogul Alexander Korda provided another model for

---

7.   In real life, the incomparable Nijinsky, dancer and choreographer, never danced again after the rupture with Diaghilev; he was 24 and he disappeared into silence and schizophrenia. Incidentally, while the Archers were making *The Red Shoes*, he was living with his wife Romola in nearby Surrey, where they had moved the year before. Richard Buckle, *Nijinsky* (Harmondsworth: Penguin, 1975), 532.

Lermontov, the Archers claimed. Korda, like Pressburger, was a Hungarian refugee from the Nazis, and had been planning a film of *The Red Shoes* as early as 1937, with Merle Oberon and Laurence Olivier; in 1948, the Archers bought back this early version of Pressburger's script, for £9,000. Finally, Michael Powell never denied – in fact in interviews he sounds proud of his reputation – that there is a lot of himself in the ruthless, sovereign producer.

The Archers assembled teams of exceptional talent in their films and never more so than for *The Red Shoes*. Numerous connections in the film evoke Stravinsky and Nijinsky's creation, *Le Sacre du Printemps* (1913), one of the greatest breakthrough achievements of modern ballet: Léonide Massine had worked on the choreography of *Sacre* for its 1919 revival, and he brought to his part as the Shoemaker the grotesque, angular dynamism and the virtuoso high leaps of his legendary predecessor; Marie Rambert, who danced in the original performance of *Sacre* in Paris, makes an appearance as herself at Vicky's matinée performance; the composer Brian Easdale's score pays tribute to Stravinsky in several passages; the film's designer Hein Heckroth, who had collaborated with the Tanztheater pioneer, Kurt Jooss, worked with the war artist Ivor Beddoes, himself a dancer and choreographer, to create a hallucinatory sequence for the passages of 'the Girl' through the dark side; her wild dance echoes above all, the fate of the Chosen Maiden in *Sacre,* prefigures the fate of Vicky Page and provides a mythic structure to the film.

The Red Shoes, like other Archers' films, moves ambiguously between far-fetched fairy tale fantasy and detailed documentary naturalism. It's a telling aspect of the Powell aesthetic, I think, that the make-up is so blatant (bushy stuck-on brows for Massine; spectacular close-ups of garish red dots in the inner corners of Moira Shearer's eyes, encircled by wild spokes and mascara'd, spiky false lashes). In *Black Narcissus* (1947), Sister Ruth (Kathleen Byron) taunts Sister Clodagh (Deborah Kerr) by painting her lips a brilliant scarlet. Lipstick and slap are colour-coded; they spell sex, desire, beauty, the artifice of art. Vicky on stage becomes herself an artefact; she's presented as a confection in a film that also proclaims itself an artefact, the product of skill and labour. As in *A Canterbury Tale* (1944), the camera unfolds traditional, local craftsmen and craftswomen at work (wheelwrights, bell-ringers, carthorse drivers, magic lanternists). In *The Red Shoes* Powell and Pressburger reveal what lies behind the art: dancers at the barre, sets being struck, chaperones knitting, and props inspected. The Archers act like those post-modern conjurors who don't pretend to disguise their trickery but enthral you with their dexterity just the same.

As is usual with the Archers' singular storytelling, the film involves us in ambiguities that after any number of viewings continue to tantalise and grip the imagination. Prominent among these questions is the conflict between 'perfection of the art and of the life'.[8] The inset Ballet represents the pinnacle of art as a highly wrought composition, but, all around this collective effort, human life is asserting its claims – as rivalry and tension, and above all, as sex and love. The impresario figure wishes to be master of it all, but ... the drama arises from the eruption of forces that elude his grip.

With *The Red Shoes*, Powell and Pressburger found in dance a supreme medium to reprise, in a different, tragic key, the struggle with primal forces. It's significant that the ballet performed at the very beginning of the film is called *Heart of Fire* (more red). Andersen, who had such mixed-up feelings about sex, avoids facing up to the erotic, but for Powell and Pressburger, it's the beating heart of the matter, which they approach through this extraordinary tour de force of innovative ballet-on-film. As Ian Christie made clear when he chose *Arrows of Desire* for the title of his splendid 1985 book about their work, the erotic lies at the centre of the Archers' search for meaning.

For the 'Ballet of The Red Shoes' Pressburger boldly condensed his source material: a superfluity of old women in the original Andersen story coalesces into the single poignant figure of the Girl's blind mother at the lit doorway, the guardian of home; the old soldier merges with the shoemaker from the original tale and when he proffers the gleaming red shoes, he recalls the malevolent queen offering Snow White the poisoned apple. The ballet introduces a figure of the Girl's Lover – danced by Robert Helpmann, who was responsible for the overall choreography (only Massine did his own). After the Shoemaker brings on the night by dropping ink on to a handkerchief and blotting out the lens, the Girl's dance carries her through a fugue of tableaux dramatizing the struggle between day and night, virtue and vice, innocence and wantonness, while the film story which frames it tilts the conflict between art and life – utter dedication to dance against love, marriage and motherhood. Lermontov expresses withering disdain for the latter with a twitch of the muscles in his right eyebrow and a curl of his lip – the phrase could have been invented to describe Walbrook's acting.

No matter that at this point of maximum tension the plot creaks, since Julian the composer has not spoken of wanting Vicky to stop dancing. Her misery catches the predicament of many women who, during the war, had been independent free spirits, eager for adventure (like Alison, the intrepid Land Girl, in *A Canterbury Tale*). This aspect must have heightened the film's meaningfulness for audiences in that era: Julian in his shiny black mac (shades of Gestapo heavy) shifts into the role of domestic oppressor, while Lermontov,

---

8.   W. B. Yeats, 'The Choice', *W. B. Yeats: Selected Poetry*: 153, ed. A. Norman Jeffares (London: Macmillan, 1968).

the tyrant who sees Vicky's greater calling, continues to recall the entertainment industry's abuses. In his case, Walbrook breathes quasi-Satanic seduction at every turn and quivers with sensual energy, but it is always suppressed (except when he smashes his fist into a mirror). The ambiguities help make the Archers' films what they are: they never let our allegiances come to rest but keep playing with our sympathies.

Does Vicky, when she plunges to her death on the railway tracks, kill herself for art... as Powell claimed? Not in her own life story as told in the film – she could have continued to dance in the Ballet Lermontov, or anywhere else, even if she had stayed married to Julian or left him for her career. The film's climax obeys the logic of myth – not the inclinations of the heart.

In Pressburger's screenplay, Lermontov thinks he has prevailed over Vicky and seen off her husband's claims. He's triumphant that she has chosen art. His devastation, intensely conveyed by Walbrook, when he tells the audience that she will not dance that night nor ever again, feels utterly genuine. Ultimately, his charisma was not strong enough against the call from below.

An original trailer for *The Red Shoes* proclaimed, 'she danced dangerously between two loves', thus stressing the rivalry between Lermontov and Julian.[9] Certainly, Vicky is tormented by the demands of the two men and is driven to flee them. But the tug of war between them isn't the primary meaning of the film. The shoes embody a wilder, deeper, Dionysiac energy that impels dance itself. She's maddened to the point of self-destruction by the overwhelming, impersonal power of this life force, which Lermontov recognises in her when he meets her for the first time and asks her, 'Why do you want to dance?' and she replies, 'Why do you want to live?' But his conception of dance demands that this force be channelled and disciplined and contained for the purposes of art. As Pressburger commented, on Desert Island Discs in 1980, his films 'deal with what is going to happen to the human values – not to the human beings themselves.'[10] The struggle in *The Red Shoes* lies between the yoke of love-in-marriage (Julian), the exactions of art (Lermontov), and the pull of wild pagan ecstasy, the zone of pleasure and sexuality; in other words, dancing subsumes her subjective self and all her emotional relations with others.[11]

---

9. *Red Shoes* (1948) [Trailer], IMDb, Home Video Trailer: Universal Pictures, https://www.imdb.com/video/vi905511193

10. *Desert Island Discs* (1980) [Radio], 'Michael Powell & Emeric Pressburger', BBC Radio 4, 20 September. https://www.bbc.co.uk/sounds/play/p009mvw8

11. See Susan Jones, 'Eliot and Dance' in *The Edinburgh Companion to T. S. Eliot and the Arts*, (eds) Frances Dickey and John D. Morgenstern Edinburgh: Edinburgh University Press) , 225–242: 231–234. Available online: http://www.jstor.com/stable/10.3366/j.ctt1bh2kwt.25

Lermontov's sexual abstinence as portrayed in this film (not a feature of his real-life models) represents sublimation in the Freudian sense, of the sex drive and the death drive into art; in Nietzschean terms, Apollo's victory over Dionysus. The discipline of the ballet is Apollonian; it checks and constrains the wilder currents in the impulse to dance. Lermontov's severity – and his seeming sexual repression – recall Angelo, in *Measure for Measure*: 'a man whose blood/Is very snow-broth ...' (Act 1 Sc. 4).

Lermontov's blood is indeed snow-broth, or rather, he would like it to remain that way. He isn't a religious hypocrite like Angelo, but the vocation of art doesn't permit wantonness and indulgence (the prima ballerina Irina is castigated for her love of parties, sweets, and late lie-ins). Yet Moira Shearer isn't an actor/dancer who conveys turbulent sexual passion; her well-bred, cool mien, pure beauty and exquisite grace make her somewhat snow-broth herself; this quality adds surprise to the madness that seizes her at the end and sharpens her torment. As in *The Rite of Spring*, in which the Chosen Maiden dances to her death, she's a blood offering to the powers below. The Archers' films often reach sweet-tempered resolutions, but *The Red Shoes* and *Black Narcissus* (1947) are ferocious dramas about Dionysiac fury taking possession of a woman.

In the novelisation Powell and Pressburger wrote thirty years later, they bring out this underlying theme: 'She [Vicky] stared at [Julian], keyed up for the performance, obsessed and unapproachable, *like one of the Greek maenads who tore Orpheus to pieces*. .... It almost seemed as if the red shoes glowed as he went out of the door.' [12]

Their film has inspired many young people to long to dance and many writers and performers to create works in response (Kate Bush, Matthew Bourne and others – a glance at the web reveals tributes from the world over, many revelling in the grue.)[13] This attraction doesn't seem to cohere with the ostensible message, that dancing is enslavement and madness and will be punished. For some, the complex seduction of sado-masochism may

---

12. Michael Powell and Emeric Pressburger, *The Red Shoes* (1978; New York: St Martin's Press, 1996), 274. My emphasis.

13. Kate Bush wrote songs for her album *The Red Shoes* (1993); she identifies strongly with Karen/the Girl/Vicky Page and brings out the erotic charge of the Archers' film: the cover image shows a foot *en pointe* in scarlet ballet pumps (and laddered tights) against a background of crashing waves, while the inside flaps spread a banquet of juicy fruits, as if by the goblins of Goblin Market, to illustrate the song, 'Eat the Music'. https://en.wikipedia.org/wiki/The_Red_Shoes_(album); Matthew Bourne devised a musical based on the film in 2016, repeated at Sadlers Wells in December 2019–January 2020, just before the first lockdown: https://www.sadlerswells.com/whats-on/2019/matthew-bournes-production-of-the-red-shoes-new-adventures/; see also *The Red Shoes* (2005), directed by Kim Yong-Gyun, https://en.wikipedia.org/wiki/The_Red_Shoes_(2005_film); and Alexis Amann's illustrations: https://www.behance.net/gallery/73910151/The-Red-Shoes-HC-Andersen

intensify the pull, as Anne Sexton wryly recognises in one of her bitter transformations of fairy tales: 'All those girls/who wore the red shoes ... /They all danced like trout on the hook …'. [14] But generally, the film embodies the mysterious power of dance as self-abandonment, as ecstasy.

The poet Paul Valéry remarked that 'a symbol is something of a time machine... It's an inconceivable compression of the time taken by operations of the spirit...' [15] Andersen's 1845 fairy tale of 'The Red Shoes' offered Michael Powell and Emeric Pressburger just such a potent symbol, a time-travelling, mythopoeic motif perfectly tuned to their cinepoetic vision and they thrillingly transfigured their morbid source into a supreme work of the modern mythic imagination.

---

14. Anne Sexton, 'The Red Shoes', in *The Complete Poems* (Boston: Houghton Mifflin, 1981), 315–17.

15. Paul Valéry, 'Mauvaises Pensées et autres', III, *Mercure de France* XXX, May 1899, in Paul Valéry, *Œuvres,* (Paris 1983), 1461.

Argentinian poster for *The Red Shoes* (1948) by Establecimento Grafico Argentina. (BFI National Archive)

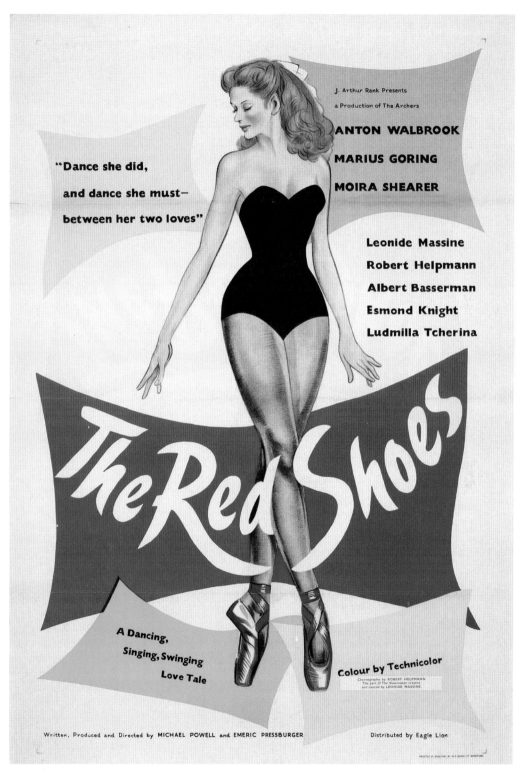

Poster for *The Red Shoes* (1948), Eagle Lion Films. (BFI National Archive)

Danish press cuttings album for
The Red Shoes (1948), compiled
for Emeric Pressburger, with artwork
by Hein Heckroth. (©Hein Heckroth/
BFI National Archive)

Cover of *Illustrated* magazine (1948) based
on a photograph by Russell Westwood.
(BFI National Archive)

Moira Shearer, photographed in costume as Victoria Page, *The Red Shoes* (1948) by Baron (Sterling Henry Nahum).
As well as working with trusted and experienced stills photographers, Powell and Pressburger enjoyed the opportunity
to work on a number of special photographic commissions for *The Red Shoes*. Baron was a prominent society
photographer, with an established practice photographing UK dance professionals. (Baron/©ITV/BFI National Archive)

173

Misty Copeland, photographed for the 70th anniversary of *The Red Shoes* (1948) for *Harper's Bazaar*, 2018, by Pari Dukovic. Copeland was one of three celebrated contemporary ballerinas photographed to mark the anniversary through an irresistible combination of fashion, film and dance. Copeland, a long-time *Red Shoes* fan, poses in an Oscar de la Renta dress with Miu Miu boots in hand – while wearing her own pair of red ballet shoes. (© Trunk Archive)

Hein Heckroth at work on 'The Ballet of the Red Shoes', *The Red Shoes* (1947) photographed by Alistair Phillips. Heckroth is shown with some of the 300 designs produced for 'The Paper Ballet': a beautiful and painterly rendering of what would become the 15-minute ballet sequence at the heart of *The Red Shoes*. Phillips was commissioned to take behind the scenes shots on *The Red Shoes*, for use in press and publicity campaigns. (Alistair Phillips/© ITV/BFI National Archive)

Production designs for 'The Ballet of the Red Shoes', *The Red Shoes* (1948) by Ivor Beddoes. Beddoes, a war artist, musician and dancer, assisted Heckroth on a hallucinatory fugue of scenes. (Ivor Beddoes/©ITV/BFI National Archive)

Production designs for 'The Ballet of the Red Shoes', *The Red Shoes* (1948) by Ivor Beddoes. The Girl leaves home and dances off into a brightly lit fairground, where she whirls past clowns, pierrots, jumping jacks, shills, and a top hatted ringmaster. She dances into a melée, spinning from partner to partner. (Ivor Beddoes/ ©ITV/BFI National Archive)

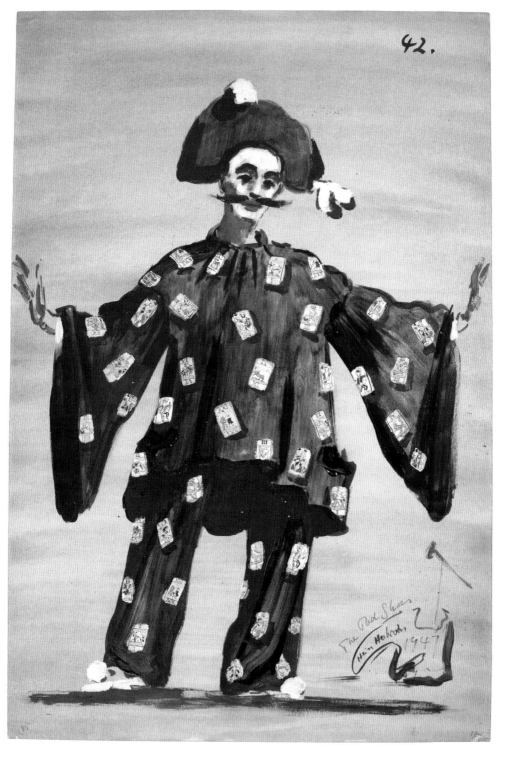

Costume design for *The Red Shoes* (1948) by Hein Heckroth. (Hein Heckroth/© ITV/Theaterwissenschaftliche Sammlung der Universität zu Köln)

Right: Dorothy Edwards (wardrobe supervisor) with Terence Morgan II (mask maker) and Elsie Withers (head of wardrobe) during costume construction for *The Red Shoes* (1948), photographed by Alistair Phillips. (Alistair Phillips/© ITV/ BFI National Archive)

Below: Production design for 'The Ballet of the Red Shoes', *The Red Shoes* (1948) by Ivor Beddoes. (Ivor Beddoes/© ITV/BFI National Archive)

Production designs for 'The Ballet of the Red Shoes', *The Red Shoes* (1948) by Ivor Beddoes. The demonic shoemaker dangles the red shoes before the Girl; his shadow falls on her, and she is compelled to dance on and on; the stage setting dissolves, the camera lifts up and away and she passes into a wide dreamscape. (Ivor Beddoes/©ITV/BFI National Archive)

Production designs for 'The Ballet of the Red Shoes', *The Red Shoes* (1948) by Hein Heckroth. (Hein Heckroth/© ITV/ La Cinémathèque française)

'The Ballet of the Red Shoes', *The Red Shoes* (1948), photographed by George Cannons. The world reasserts its claims on the Girl: it's night, and she is swallowed up in a bacchanal of daubed and masked figures, part shaman, part monster, part skeleton (chiefly Beddoes' work). Cannons was employed as a photographer alongside Alistair Phillips, Cornel Lucas and George Courtney Ward. It was typical for more than one photographer to work on a production, but this unusually high number of experienced stills professionals signals the substantial investment made in the film's publicity campaign. (George Cannons/© ITV/BFI National Archive)

The nightmare sequence in 'The Ballet of the Red Shoes', *The Red Shoes* (1948) photographed by George Cannons. (George Cannons/© ITV/BFI National Archive)

The nightmare sequence in 'The Ballet of the Red Shoes', *The Red Shoes* (1948) photographed by George Cannons. (George Cannons/© ITV/BFI National Archive)

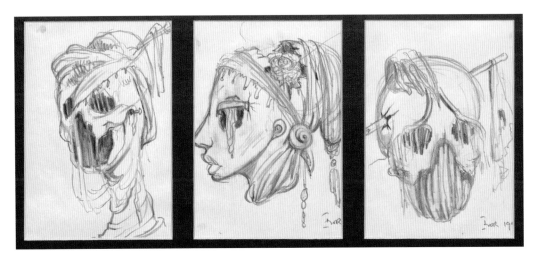

Designs for the nightmare sequence in 'The Ballet of the Red Shoes', *The Red Shoes* (1948) by Ivor Beddoes, whose experiences as a war artist shaped his vision. (Ivor Beddoes/© ITV/BFI National Archive)

Design for the nightmare sequence in 'The Ballet of the Red Shoes', *The Red Shoes* (1948) by Ivor Beddoes.
(Ivor Beddoes/©ITV/BFI National Archive)

Mask maker, Terence Morgan II, with a number of the realised masks for the nightmare sequence in 'The Ballet of the Red Shoes', *The Red Shoes* (1948). Photographed by Alistair Phillips. (Alistair Phillips/© ITV/BFI National Archive)

Production designs for 'The Ballet of the Red Shoes', *The Red Shoes* (1948) by Hein Heckroth (top) and Ivor Beddoes (above). Towards the end of 'The Ballet of the Red Shoes', the camera lifts and we are on stage, watching Vicky back in her own story as she pirouettes dazzlingly to Julian's baton and Lermontov's command. (Hein Heckroth/© ITV/ BFI National Archive; Ivor Beddoes/© ITV/BFI National Archive)

Right: Sketch ('scribble') by Hein Heckroth,
with note by Ivor Beddoes, illuminating their
working process, *The Red Shoes* (1948).
(Ivor Beddoes/©ITV/BFI National Archive)

Below: Production design for 'The Ballet
of the Red Shoes', *The Red Shoes* (1948)
by Hein Heckroth. (Hein Heckroth/©ITV/
La Cinémathèque française)

187

Léonide Massine, photographed in character as the Shoemaker, *The Red Shoes* (1948) by Baron (Sterling Henry Nahum). (Baron/© ITV/BFI National Archive)

Production design for 'The Ballet of the Red Shoes', *The Red Shoes* (1948) by Ivor Beddoes. (Ivor Beddoes/© ITV/ BFI National Archive)

Production design for 'The Ballet of the Red Shoes', *The Red Shoes* (1948) by Hein Heckroth. (Hein Heckroth/© ITV/ La Cinémathèque française)

Notes from a Milliner

Stephen Jones

I first came across *The Red Shoes* (1948) in 1976 at St Martin's School of Art, where I was studying fashion. Our tutor, Marit Allen (famed costume designer of *White Mischief, Brokeback Mountain* – and the *Thunderbirds* movie, on which we collaborated), was our part-time complementary studies tutor. In Film Club she wowed us with Fellini's *Juliet of the Spirits* – 'Sponsored by Bri-Nylon' – nectar to us punks. The following week's class featured a scratched and dusty print of *The Red Shoes*. Instantly I was seduced by the lush colour of the opening scenes, the mind-blowing set design, the creativity of the surrealist ballet and the central theme of 'Life or Art' – so pertinent to a young fashion designer wrestling with the vicissitudes and complexities of my newly chosen career. In the Nineties, I bought the VHS, then later, multiple DVDs, and finally downloaded it from the internet. Each time seduced and drowning in its heady beauty.

In the autumn of 2006, somehow my obsession with the film syncing with the cycles of fashion, led me to create a collection based on *The Red Shoes*. By then, I had almost learnt the script word for word – even perfecting Moira Shearer's received pronunciation: 'Julian, take off the Red Shoes'. I knew each individual colour and flickering movement across the screen and had fallen in love with Lermontov, played by the elegant Anton Walbrook, in particular his fabulous wardrobe. Each element of the film was an inspiration, the visual

---

Opposite: 'Ecstasy', 2007, by Stephen Jones. (© Stephen Jones/Collection of the artist)

and aural motifs, the rollercoaster of overwrought emotions and its element of camp. From these, I extracted sixteen haute couture hats for my Spring and Summer 2007 collection named *Artifice*. Highlights were, 'Double Entendre', a hand-painted transparent turquoise visor, mimicking the floating, coloured theatre gels from the beginning section of the ballet. 'Smashed', a broken-mirror headdress inspired by the scene where Lermontov has just punched a mirror, having lost Vicky; 'Ecstasy', a photoprint of Vicki's extravagantly painted eyes as she descends into madness … or is it elation? And of course, a tableau-hat comprising a pair of miniature red satin ballet slippers mounted on a silk stage, adorned with the gilded red velvet drapes of the Royal Opera House in London's Covent Garden.

Forty years on from when I first saw the film, a scene between the Svengali Lermontov and the student Vicki repeats itself to me almost daily:

LERMONTOV: Why do you want to dance?
VICKI: Why do you want to live?
LERMONTOV: I don't know exactly why … I must.

And this, dear reader, is the question I try to resolve every day with a hat.

Opposite: 'Life Or Art', 2007, by Stephen Jones. (© Stephen Jones/Collection of the artist)

The Contributors

With new photography by Nigel Arthur and David Briggs.

Ian Christie has written and curated extensively about the work of Powell and Pressburger, starting with a 1978 book and BFI retrospective, which led to a long involvement with Martin Scorsese. His other main field of activity has been the early Soviet avant-garde, with a new film about Eisenstein, *A Trip to Tetlapayac* (2023). He is Professor of Film and Media History at Birkbeck, University of London.

Sarah Greenwood is an Academy Award-nominated and BAFTA award-winning Production Designer. She has worked regularly with director Joe Wright on films including *Cyrano* (2021), *Darkest Hour* (2017), *Atonement* (2007) and *Pride & Prejudice* (2005). Her other films include *Sherlock Holmes* (2009), *Beauty and the Beast* (2017) and *Barbie* (2023). She collaborates closely with Katie Spencer, her long-time Set Decorator.

Alexandra Harris is the author of *Romantic Moderns* (2010), *Weatherland* (2015), *Time and Place* (2019), and many essays on art, literature, and landscape. She is Professor of English at the University of Birmingham, where she founded the 'Arts of Place' research network, and a Fellow of the Royal Society of Literature.

Joanna Hogg is a celebrated film director and screenwriter who lives in London, UK. Her feature films include *Unrelated* (2007), *Archipelago* (2010), *Exhibition* (2013), *The Souvenir* (2019), *The Souvenir Part II* (2020) and *The Eternal Daughter* (2022).

Stephen Jones burst on to the London fashion scene during its explosion of street style in the late seventies. By 1980, Jones had opened his first millinery salon in the heart of London's Covent Garden. Over forty years later, Jones's era-defining edge continues to attract a celebrity clientele which includes, Rihanna, Lady Gaga, Mick Jagger, and the Princesses. His beguiling hats routinely grace the most celebrated magazine covers and catwalks around the world.

Caitlin McDonald works at the University of Dundee, where she completed her PhD research on the screenplays and novels of Emeric Pressburger. Her research interests include national cinema and identity, exile cinema, and unfinished films. She is currently working on an article examining the legacy of Nazism in Pressburger's unmade films.

Nathalie Morris is a writer, film historian and curator. She has held senior curatorial positions at the BFI National Archive and the Academy Museum of Motion Pictures, and has organised exhibitions on many aspects of cinema history including the art of the Hollywood backdrop, Indian cinema posters, Women and Silent Britain, and British Hitchcock.

Sandy Powell OBE is an Academy Award-winning costume designer who has collaborated with filmmakers including Derek Jarman, Martin Scorsese, Sally Potter, Neil Jordan and Todd Haynes. Her extensive credits include *Caravaggio* (1986), *Orlando* (1992), *Far From Heaven* (2002), *Gangs of New York* (2002), *The Young Victoria* (2009), *Cinderella* (2015), *Carol* (2015) and *The Favourite* (2018). In 2023 she became the first film costume designer to be awarded the prestigious BAFTA Fellowship.

Mahesh Rao is a novelist and short story writer. His short fiction has been shortlisted for various awards, including the Commonwealth Short Story Prize. His work has appeared in numerous publications, including *The New York Times*, *Prospect*, *The Baffler*, *Vogue* and *Elle*. His most recent novel, *Polite Society*, was published in 2019.

Thelma Schoonmaker Powell is a three-time Academy Award winning editor, having worked for more than forty years alongside filmmaker Martin Scorsese. In 2019 she was honoured with a BAFTA Fellowship, the highest honour that BAFTA can bestow. In addition to her film editing, Schoonmaker Powell works tirelessly to promote the films and writings of her late husband, Michael Powell.

Claire Smith is Senior Curator of Special Collections at the BFI National Archive, where she curates filmmakers' paper archives, the photographic and graphic arts collections. She has published with the V&A Museum, The Henry Moore Foundation, Royal Academy, Courtauld Institute and BFI, as well as conducting research for exhibitions across these organisations.

Sarah Street is Professor of Film at the University of Bristol. She has published extensively on aspects of British cinema, and also on film colour histories, technologies and aesthetics. Her latest book is *Colour Films in Britain: The Eastmancolor Revolution* (Bloomsbury/BFI, 2021), and she is Principal Investigator on STUDIOTEC: Film Studios: Infrastructure, Culture, Innovation in Britain, France, Germany and Italy, 1930–60, a project funded by the European Research Council.

Tilda Swinton is an Academy Award and BAFTA award winning actor, known for her diverse portfolio of work across theatre, art, independent and mainstream cinema, and her chameleonic ability to inhabit a role. She has collaborated with directors including Derek Jarman, Sally Potter, Jim Jarmusch, Bong Joon-Ho, Wes Anderson, Apichatpong Weerasethakul and Joanna Hogg, and is a longstanding advocate for Powell and Pressburger's cinema.

Tim Walker's photographs have entranced the readers of *Vogue* for over a decade. Extravagant staging and romantic motifs characterise his unmistakable style. At the age of twenty-five he shot his first fashion story for *Vogue*, and has photographed for the British, Italian, and American editions, as well as *W* and *LOVE* magazines ever since.

Marina Warner is a writer of fiction and non-fiction, history and criticism; her books include *From the Beast to the Blonde* (1994) and *Stranger Magic: Charmed States & the Arabian Nights* (2011) and her essays have been collected in *Signs & Wonders* (1994) and *Forms of Enchantment: Writings on Art and Artists* (2018). She wrote *L'Atalante* for BFI Classics, and contributes regularly to the *New York Review of Books* and the *London Review of Books*.

Michelle Williams Gamaker is an artist filmmaker based in London. Her works explore *fictional activism*, which revisits the problems of casting and restages scenes from twentieth-century British and Hollywood studio, by using the tools (and magic) of cinema against itself to exorcise cinematic ghosts. Williams Gamaker was joint-winner of FLAMIN's Jarman Award in 2020 and recipient of a British Academy Wolfson Fellowship in 2022. She is a Reader in Fine Art at Goldsmiths.

Editors' Acknowledgements

I n the spirit of the Archers, the development of this publication has been a truly collaborative effort. Special thanks to our contributors, and to BFI colleagues who have shared their research around Powell and Pressburger so openly; particularly Carolyne Beavan – who has spent many years cataloguing the rich and voluminous papers of both Emeric Pressburger and Michael Powell – as well as Robin Baker, James Bell, Sonja Genaity, Frances Iddon, Fiona Maxwell and Steve Tollervey. To Nigel Arthur, Nigel Good and David Briggs for their skilled digitisation of works on paper; to Storm Patterson for her editorial wizardry; and to our curatorial colleagues for their support and feedback. To our many wonderful partners, estates, archives and Archers' families who have long progressed a wider understanding of Powell and Pressburger's cinema: Andrew and Kevin Macdonald; Thelma Schoonmaker Powell; Fiona Williams and Marc Berlin; Niki and Mason Cardiff; Julia Dunn; Christian and Jodi Heckroth; Sylvia Junge; and Frankie Shrapnel. To our publishing colleagues – Rebecca Barden, Anna Coatman and Tom Cabot – who have shared our vision. And to those who may not appear in name within the publication, but on whose knowledge and understanding our research stands, including the work of Charles Barr, Pam Cook, Steve Crook, Kevin Gough-Yates, Stella Hockenhull, Pamela Hutchinson and Andrew Moor. Nathalie would like to offer a second, and grateful, thanks to Charles Barr for his comments on the final manuscript. She would also like to thank David Charles for his love and support while working on this project, and Wilfred Charles, who was born during its early stages (thanks, Wilfred, for all those helpful naps!). Claire would like to thank Emma and Lucy Smith-Coombs, for their insights into what our youngest readers might appreciate. To Peter Coombs, for always being there. And, to Rob Smith, who has offered his time and expertise so generously, and has helped to make this long-cherished project a reality during the challenges of a global pandemic. To these people and our friends and families who have shared this journey with us, a huge thank you.

Index